AFRICAN URBAN KINSMEN

African
Urban Kinsmen

The Ga of Central Accra

by MARION KILSON

ST. MARTIN'S PRESS

NEW YORK

For Marion Greene and Emily Dusser de Barenne

AFFILIATED PUBLISHERS: Macmillan Limited, London
—also at Bombay, Calcutta, Madras and Melbourne

CONTENTS

ILLUSTRATIONS

FIGURES

TABLES

PREFACE

This limited ethnographic study concerning the social and cultural life of a community of traditional African townsmen is based upon fieldwork conducted in Ghana during ten months in 1964—5. In this monograph I am primarily concerned with aspects of the kinship system of the Ga people living in Central Accra including their residential and life crisis ceremonial patterns. I regard this study as complementary to *Kpele Lala: Ga Religious Songs and Symbols* which analyses the major traditional religious cult of the Ga people and is based primarily upon research done during three months in 1968. I, therefore, do not discuss extensively cosmological conceptions or traditional religious ideas, roles, and practices that have been reported either in *Kpele Lala* or in articles in the *Journal of Religion in Africa*.

During the decade that this monograph has been in process from its origin as a doctoral dissertation, I have been indebted to many people for assistance at different phases in the development of the study. Among the individuals and institutions in Ghana and the United States which made this study possible, I wish to thank a few for their special kindness and consideration. Professor T. O. Beidelman has given me invaluable advice, criticism, and encouragement from the initial planning stage onwards. Professor John Whiting, as my thesis supervisor, introduced me to the computer age. Mrs. Wilma K. Kerby-Miller, then Dean of Women in Harvard University, generously provided funds from the Charles E. Merrill Trust Fund to cover almost all research expenses. Mr. Thomas Hodgkin, then Director of the Institute of African Studies, at the University of Ghana, made available both facilities at the Institute and supplementary research funds. Support for writing was provided initially by a predoctoral grant from the National Institutes of Health (1-F1-MH-29, 380-0/BEH) and later by the Radcliffe Institute. In the field, my research assistants, Miss Gladys Adjei, Mr. James Amon Kotey, and Miss Juliana Alote, gave me invaluable assistance in collecting data. Dr. Ana Livia Cordero and Miss Angelina Yawson, then staff members at the James Town Maternity Clinic, not only introduced me to Central Accra but made available their social survey data to me. The Ghana Department of Statistics kindly permitted me to use unpublished census data. My debt to certain Ga individuals is incalculable, for their generosity not only in the hours which we spent together but in the knowledge which they shared with me; I am especially grateful to Mr. E. A. Ammah, Mme. Yoomo Dantserebi, and Mr. Henry Amoo Adjei. I am appreciative of Martin Kilson's insistence that the thesis should become a book. Finally, my most personal debt is to him and Jenny, Peter, and Hannah Kilson who endure the inconveniences of a part-time wife-mother on both sides of the Atlantic. Without the generosity and patience of each of these individuals, this monograph could not have been completed.

I also wish to acknowledge my appreciation to the editor of the *Ghana Journal of Sociology* for permitting me to use materials originally published in that journal.

Newton College
January 1974

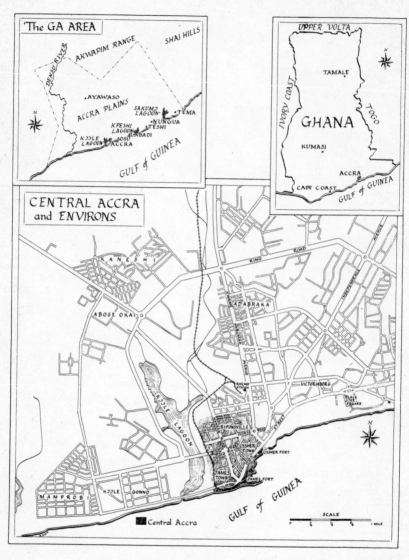

Map of Central Accra, the Ga Area, Ghana.

INTRODUCTION

Central Accra is a densely populated, active, noisy centre of African urban life in the heart of the national capital of Ghana.[1] Visually Central Accra is white and rust-brown: white buildings with rusting roofs set on laterite soil; occasionally a green tree top rises above the wall of a compound. Houses are built close together, particularly in the oldest area of settlement adjacent to the seaside forts. The entrances to many houses open onto narrow dusty lanes rather than onto paved streets. Sometimes the spacious homes of professional Africans abut the small tin-roofed houses of traders and fishermen. The principal streets are lined by small African enterprises which frequently advertise their commodities and services pictorially rather than graphically. A large alarm clock or wrist watch on the wall of a watch repairer's shop proclaims his trade to potential customers, while the image of a man drinking a glass of beer on the wall of a bar announces the refreshment to be found inside. Women traders either walk through the streets carrying their wares on their heads or sit outside their houses at small tables which display commodities, such as *kenkey*, tomatoes, combs, cigarettes, and candy. Fishermen sit outside their houses mending nets and conversing. Small children fetch water from street corner standpipes. In mid-afternoon clusters of uniformed school children wander homewards; later civil servants return from work either on foot or by bus. In the late afternoon mothers bathe their small children either on the curbside or inside their compounds. Frequently, a street is closed to motor traffic so that the mourners at a funeral may sit outside the house under the shade of a large tarpaulin. The area is scarcely ever silent — far into the night the flickering kerosene lamps of traders illuminate clusters of people laughing and conversing; the partial stillness of the night is broken by the clank of pails at the standpipes long before dawn.

A visitor walking through the byways of Central Accra for the first time senses that he might be in any comparable residential area of marginal élites and manual labourers in any West African capital. The smells, sights, and sounds which he encounters are as characteristic of Treicheville in Abidjan or Ginger Hall in Freetown as they are of Central Accra: the deep open trash-filled gutters, the sizzling smell of frying plantain, the occasional whiff of urine, the small open shops of

Central Accra.

artisans, the barber cutting hair under a tree, children chasing home-made wheel toys, men playing checkers in the shade of a house, women carrying sleeping infants on their backs and possessions on their heads, the sharp clank of aluminium pails, the reprimanding shouts of mothers, the rhythm of highlife pulsating from an open window, the warm laughter of good fellowship. Nevertheless, these superficial sensory similarities mask wide cultural and social variations in the lives of the inhabitants of such urban areas.

Within Central Accra live representatives of diverse ethnic groups who participate in the modern industrial economy of the city primarily in lower socio-economic categories, as clerks, midwives, teachers, barbers, traders, manual labourers, and fishermen. Many inhabitants of Central Accra were born in other parts of Ghana and West Africa and have come to the city to seek their fortunes. Like migrants elsewhere, they have sought to adapt to the unfamiliar urban environment through such institutions as mutual aid societies based on ethnic affiliations or churches. Some migrants aspire to return to their natal lands, others hope to become permanent urban dwellers. The aspirations, social networks, and domestic arrangements of comparable migrant populations in other African cities have received considerable attention in the sociological literature of recent years.[2]

My concern is not with such newcomers to the city but with the traditional townsmen of Central Accra. For generations Central Accra has been the home of an urban population around which the modern city has developed and among whom migrants have settled. The members of this core population are Ga-speaking people who not only constitute the majority of the inhabitants of Central Accra, but are true townsmen in the sense that their social relations are fully encompassed by the urban centre.[3] Nevertheless, the stable continuity of the Ga population and its relatively undifferentiated socio-economic attributes have facilitated the persistence of aspects of their traditional social system which are not associated directly with the urban industrial complex, especially their kinship system. Consequently, in this book I consider the continuing relevance of traditional kinship conceptions and institutions and suggest aspects of the relation between ideas and institutional change within the Ga community of Central Accra. The first chapter provides the historical and demographic background of the Ga community in Central Accra; the second analyses the basic conceptions and institutions of Ga kinship; the third discusses the relationship between these ideas and contemporary residential units; the fourth concerns the ways in which kinship conceptions and networks are maintained through life crisis ceremonies, and the fifth explores factors affecting adherence to traditional cultural conceptions of individuals who live within a community of kinsmen situated within the confines of a modern African city.

REFERENCES

1. Accra is located at 5°31′ N, 0°11′ W on the Gulf of Guinea (see map). Throughout this study I use the ethnographic present to refer to the time of my field work in Accra during the middle and late 1960s.
2. e.g., Michael Banton, *West African City*, London, 1957; Remi Clignet and Frank Jordan, 'Urbanization and Social Differentiation in Africa', *Cahiers d'Études Africaines 11*, 1971, pp. 261—97; A. L. Epstein, *Politics in an Urban African Community*, Manchester, 1958 and 'The Network and Urban Social Organization', *Human Problems in British Central Africa 29*, 1961, pp. 29—62; Max Gluckman, 'Anthropological Problems Arising from the African Industrial Revolution', in Aidan Southall (ed.), *Social Change in Modern Africa*, London, 1961, pp. 67—82; Josef Gugler, 'Life in a Dual System: Eastern Nigerians in Towns, 1961', *Cahiers d'Études Africaines 11*, 1971, pp. 400—21; W. D. Hammond-Tooke, 'Urbanization and the Interpretation of Misfortune', *Africa 40*, 1970, pp. 25—39; Kenneth Little, *West African Urbanization*, Cambridge, 1965; Phillip Mayer, *Townsmen or Tribesmen*, Cape Town, 1961, and 'Migrancy and the Study of Africans in Towns', *American Anthropologist 64*, 1962, pp. 576—92; J. Clyde Mitchell, *The Kalela Dance*, Manchester, 1956; Monica Wilson and Archie Mareje, *Langa*, Cape Town, 1963.

3. Mayer 1962: 580. The Ga homeland is the Accra Plains of southeastern Ghana which extend along the Atlantic coast for about forty miles, and are bounded by the Akwapim scarp on the north. The more transitory eastern and western boundaries are recognised conventionally as the Laloi Lagoon and the Densu River, respectively. The Ga language belongs to the Kwa sub-family of Niger-Congo. The Kwa languages are distributed along the West African coast from western Liberia to eastern Nigeria (Joseph H. Greenberg, *The Languages of Africa*, Bloomington, 1966, pp. 8, 173). Within the Kwa group, Ga is a member of the 'Ga-Adangme cluster. The other dialects of this cluster are Ada, Osudoku, Krobo, Shai and the various types of the Adangme spoken at Kpone, Prampram and Ningo.' (Vincent Okunor, *Tone in the Ga Verb*, Legon, 1967, p.i). While Adangme speakers represent the 'eastern neighbours' of the Ga people, their neighbours to the north, the Akwapim, and to the west, the Awutu, speak dialects of Twi-Fante (ibid.: ii). Moreover, 'Ga has been considerably influenced by Twi-Fante' (ibid.). The bibliography includes references to the literature on the Ga people and on Accra.

CHAPTER I

THE GA IN CENTRAL ACCRA

Since the origins of the Ga community in Central Accra antedate historical records, precise knowledge of the initial settlement may never be known. Nevertheless, by integrating information drawn from ethnohistorical, archaeological, and historical sources, it is possible to outline several major factors effecting the transformation of a sparsely populated Ga fishing hamlet or hamlets into a densely populated multi-ethnic residential community of marginal élites, manual laborers and traders within an industrial urban unit. These factors include the establishment of trading relations between Ga and European merchants in the sixteenth century, the Akwamu destruction of Great Accra in 1677, the transfer of the capital of the Gold Coast Colony to Accra in 1877, and the continuing growth of Accra as the national centre of administration and economic distribution in subsequent years.

Although Central Accra has been a *locus* of Ga political authority for almost three hundred years, the first Ga capital known in historic times was Great Accra or Ayawaso, situated some eleven miles from the coast on the edge of the Akwapim scarp. According to Ga tradition, the Ga migrated from the east into their present area: some came overland and settled at Ayawaso, others came by sea and settled on the coast at the site of modern Central Accra. Subsequently, the Ga left Ayawaso for coastal Accra.[1] Although recent archaeological and historical research supports the basic validity of these traditions, the reality which these investigations describe is more complex. Archaeological evidence suggests that the ethnic composition of the Accra Plains has been the same for hundreds of years. 'A belt of five or ten miles along the coast has certainly been well populated for a great deal more than a thousand years, probably for the most part by the Ga-Adangme people.'[2]

The earliest European records refer to the inland town of Great Accra, whose ruler had authority over the coastal trade.[3] Recent research suggests that the commercial importance of Great Accra antedates European penetration of the coast. In pre-European times, Great Accra probably was an important centre of the overland gold trade and the small coastal settlements may have engaged in overseas trade with the Bights of Benin.[4] With the advent of European merchants, the flow of gold changed from the east to the south, but the settlement pattern and trade centres remained the same.

> Each trade-path ... was similarly organized. A line of small towns seems to have extended along the coastal belt. At a distance of half a day's journey inland lay an important town – Agona, Great Accra, and Shai. A further fifteen miles inland were the large markets for the interchange of imports and of the gold, *aggrey* and slaves of the forest.[5]

By the mid-seventeenth century, Accra had become 'the greatest gold market on the Gold Coast.'[6] In order to achieve and maintain this position, Great Accra had to have control over the trade routes to the forest and to the coast.

> Within the northern boundaries of the Accra state, near the modern Nsawam, there flourished a large market known as Abonse. Abonse was referred to as a 'free market', which meant that the King of Accra permitted any traders from the interior to come there in safety to barter their goods. Such visitors, on the other hand, were not allowed to proceed beyond Abonse; from Abonse to the Accra capital, and from the capital to the beaches, trade was exclusively in the hands of the Accras.[7]

On the coast five European powers (Denmark, England, Holland, Portugal and Sweden) competed for the gold and slaves of the Ga traders.[8]

The prosperity and authority of Great Accra ended abruptly with its destruction by the Akwamu in 1677.[9] Some Ga escaped to coastal Accra where they retained control until their final defeat in 1681.[10] For the following fifty years, the Ga state was a province within the Akwamu empire. When the Ga polity resumed its independent status in 1730, the capital of the state, which was now limited to the Accra Plains, was coastal Accra, the site of contemporary Central Accra. 'In this way the humble fishing villages which the Portuguese saw from their ships in the 1470s developed into the capital of the Accra people, and in time, ... have become the capital of the independent Republic of Ghana.'[11]

With the Akwamu defeat of the Ga, the population of coastal Accra began to assume its cosmopolitan character. Representatives of diverse tribal groups came there to participate in the overseas trade. Some settled permanently and became assimilated to Ga cultural standards; in time their descendants became identified as Ga. In contemporary Central Accra, Ga distinguish between 'true Ga (*Ganyo krong*)' and other Ga. The former are descendants of the Ga who in the mid-seventeenth century lived either on the coast or at the inland town of Ayawaso; the latter are descendants of latter immigrant non-Ga settlers. Ga attribute the founding of the seven quarters of Central Accra in part to the settlement of immigrant communities and in part to the fission of established units. According to tradition, the true Ga settled in the Asere quarter. Political disputes within Asere led to the establishment of the Gbese, Sempe, and Akumadze quarters. The three other quarters, however, were founded by immigrants: Otublohum by Akwamu, Abola by Fanti, Ngleshi Alata by Nigerians. Within each of the Central Accra quarters today are Ga families whose ancestors are said to have been non-Ga immigrants.

The development of Accra as a modern urban centre has been dependent upon its commercial and administrative functions. Accra has been an important commercial centre from the time of earliest European contact. 'Its fortunes declined somewhat with the abolition of the slave trade at the beginning of the nineteenth century and the substitution of trade in natural produce like palm oil, kernels, rubber and kola. The ports of Ada and Prampram ... provided more convenient outlets for this trade.'[12] Initially trade within Ghana was the responsibility of African merchants. Toward the end of the nineteenth century, however, African business declined with the decision of European firms 'to send out more European agents, so paving the way for the establishment of part-retail, part-wholesale European-managed stores'.[13] Accra, however, continued to flourish as a commercial centre and port until 1959, when the new harbour was opened at Tema. Accra, nevertheless, retains its significance as a major centre of economic distribution in contemporary Ghana. Moreover, in recent years the city 'has become the leading manufacturing centre in the nation'.[14]

Accra assumed its administrative role when the capital of the Gold Coast Colony was transferred from Cape Coast to Accra in 1877. The ostensible reason for the change was that the climate was drier and healthier in Accra than in Cape Coast. Probably the unruliness of the territory to the east of Accra was instrumental in this decision. 'In 1855, the Governor, in a despatch to the Secretary of State, wrote that the country lying to the east of Christiansborg was more disorderly and uncivilised and less disposed to British Government than any other part of Ghana.'[15] In subsequent years, governmental requirements and functions have assumed an increasingly significant role in the economy and geographical development of Accra.

Until the beginning of the twentieth century, the territorial extent of Accra was confined primarily to the traditional Ga settlement along the coast between Ussher Fort and Kǫǫle Lagoon.[16] The enlargement of the European community in the late nineteenth century led to the establishment of a separate European residential area at Victoriaborg.

The bubonic plague of 1908 resulted in the founding of African communities at Adabraka and Koọle Gonno. Overcrowding in the old African settlement around Ussher and James Town forts led to the expansion of its northern boundaries during the first quarter of the century. The building of the railway led to the extension of the African community along the present Kwame Nkrumah Avenue. During the period after the Second World War, the built-up area of Accra has increased tremendously. In 1956 this area was 'forty square miles, with extensions beyond it to the north and east'.[17] The spatial growth of Accra is reflected in the extensions of the municipal boundaries which in 1896 incorporated Ussher Town, James Town, and Osu; the boundaries were extended to include Labadi, Nungua and Teshi in 1945, and Tema in 1963.[18] The present municipal boundaries, therefore, incorporate the greater part of the area of the post-Akwamu Ga state.

Population increments have paralelled geographical extensions. In 1837, the mulatto missionary, Freeman, estimated the population of Accra as 'not less than ten or twelve thousand'.[19] According to Government censuses, the African population of Accra was 16,267 in 1891; 14,842 in 1901; 15,313 in 1911; 38,049 in 1921; 60,726 in 1931; 133,192 in 1948, and 337,828 in 1960.[20] Although these figures indicate the overall growth of Accra, particularly in the past fifty years, they do not show the growth within specific areas of the city. Some comparative data, however, are available on the population growth within Central Accra during the past seventy years (see Table I/1). These figures show that while the total population of a geographically expanding Accra has increased more than twenty-fold, it has not even doubled within the old area of African urban settlement. Moreover, these figures overestimate the population growth within Central Accra, for the territorial extent of the units which the censuses label Ussher Town and James Town is less in 1910 than in 1960.

The demographic attributes of the contemporary Ga population in Central Accra reflect both the continuity and stability of this

TABLE I/1
POPULATION OF CENTRAL ACCRA*

Year	Male	Female	Total
1891	7,917	8,350	16, 267
1901	6,891	7,951	14, 842
1960	12,613	13,274	25,887

*Government Documents 1891:42, 1902:20, and 1960 census schedules.

population and the socio-economic consequences of its strategic coastal location during historic times.[21] In the 1960 Ghana census, Central Accra comprises sixty-seven enumeration areas which incorporate the old coastal Ga settlement around the forts and its northern extensions (see map). Before the opening of the port at Tema in 1959 and the development of a new retail centre north of the railway depot, Central Accra was the centre of commercial life in Accra; today Central Accra is primarily an African residential and trading centre.

The continuity and stability of the Ga population is reflected in its demographic profiles which contrast vividly with those of the non-Ga population in Central Accra. In 1960, Ga constituted 58 per cent of the total population of Central Accra and 54 per cent of the adult population.[22] Ga males accounted for 53 per cent of the male population and 44 per cent of the adult male population, while Ga females comprised 64 per cent of both the female and adult female populations. While the Ga population is predominantly non-migrant (91 per cent), the non-Ga population is predominantly migrant (73 per cent). The sex and age profiles of the non-Ga population accord with those of migrant urban populations, whereas those of the Ga population are consistent with a settled urban population (see Table I/2).[23] Thus, while non-Ga men exceed non-Ga women, Ga women exceed Ga men in Central Accra. Whereas the age profiles for non-Ga of both sexes show a disproportionately large number of persons in economically productive age categories (i.e., 15—44 years), comparable age profiles for Ga depict a relatively balanced age distribution. The difference in mobility between Ga and non-Ga populations in Central Accra, therefore, explains in large measure differences in the demographic attributes of the two populations.

During the era of British colonial rule, the strategic coastal location of the Ga people facilitated their participation in western religious, educational, and administrative institutions, especially after the transfer of the capital of the Gold Coast Colony to Accra in 1877. Consequently, the proportion of Ga who are Christian, educated, and who occupy skilled western occupational categories exceeds that of other Ghanaian peoples (see Table I/3). The majority of Ga, however, are not well educated by western standards and participate in the national economy either as fishermen and farmers or as unskilled labourers.

Within the Ga population of Central Accra, there is a considerable difference between the educational and occupational profiles of men and women (see Table I/4). Whereas the majority of men have had at least a middle school education, only a fifth of the women have enjoyed corresponding educational opportunities. Slightly more than a quarter of the male population is engaged in some white-collar occupation; a fifth pursue the traditional coastal occupation of

TABLE I/2

AGE STRUCTURE OF GA AND NON-GA POPULATIONS, CENTRAL ACCRA, 1960

Population	Age Groups									
	0–1	1–4	5–9	10–14	15–24	25–44	45–64	65+	Total	N
	%	%	%	%	%	%	%	%	%	
Ga										
Total	4	15	14	13	18	20	11	5	100	36,239
Male	5	16	15	13	19	19	9	4	100	16,100
Female	4	14	14	13	17	20	12	6	100	20,139
Non-Ga										
Total	3	11	12	9	24	32	8	1	100	25,895
Male	3	10	8	6	26	36	10	1	100	14,423
Female	4	12	16	12	22	28	5	1	100	11,472

TABLE I/3
EDUCATIONAL AND ÉLITE OCCUPATIONAL STATISTICS FOR GHANAIAN AND GA POPULATIONS, 1960

Education	Total over 6 years			Past		Present	
	Never	Past	Present	Middle School	Secondary School	Middle School	Secondary School
	%	%	%	%	%	%	%
Ghana							
Males	63.4	18.1	18.5	62	6	28.2	3.6
Females	83.0	7.4	9.6	43.8	3.3	22.2	1.5
Ga							
Males	30.7	36.3	33.0	67.8	13.9	30.1	8.7
Females	60.6	16.7	22.7	65.0	4.3	30.1	3.9

Élite Occupation*	Male	Female
Ghana	6.5	1.5
Ga	21.0	5.6

*i.e., professional, administrative and clerical occupational categories.

TABLE I/4
EDUCATIONAL AND OCCUPATIONAL STATISTICS FOR GA IN CENTRAL ACCRA, 1960

Item	Male	Female	N
	%	%	
Education (over 15 years)			
No schooling	28	72	10,307
Primary school	7	6	1,188
Middle school	52	20	5,981
Secondary school	13	2	1,149
Total	100	100	18,625
Occupation			
Professional/Administrative	8	2	567
Clerical	20	4	1,287
Sales	5	83	6,221
Fishing	21	—	1,036
Labourer	39	11	2,705
Other	7	—	365
Total	100	100	12,181

fisherman, and the remainder are engaged in some manual occupation. By contrast, the overwhelming proportion of Ga women are engaged in trading (83 per cent) and only 6 per cent in white-collar occupations. From the perspective of occupational categories, therefore, the Ga population of Central Accra constitutes a stable community of manual labourers, traders, and marginal élites.

Although comparative occupational statistics for the Ga and non-Ga populations of Central Accra are not available, interesting variations exist in the educational profiles of these populations. While a higher proportion of Ga men have had some western education than non-Ga men, slightly fewer Ga women have been educated than non-Ga women (see Table I/5). Moreover, a slightly higher proportion of Ga women (61 per cent) than non-Ga women (51 per cent) are employed; this difference probably is related to the high proportion of Ga women traders in Accra.[24]

While these socio-economic data are not sufficiently detailed to formulate precise hypotheses about the selective factors determining population movements into and out of Central Accra, some inferences may be made. The age and sex profiles and socio-economic data for the Ga suggest that there may be a tendency for highly skilled adult males born in Accra to move out of Central Accra either to the suburbs of Accra or to other industrial urban units, leaving behind a relatively less well-educated, older, female population in the homeland, which in this case is Central Accra and not some rural village. At the same time, however, Central Accra is an initial residential area for Ga born in other parts of the Ga area who migrate to Accra. Such an explanation would

TABLE I/5
EDUCATIONAL STATISTICS FOR CENTRAL ACCRA, 1960

Population	Aged 6–14 years			Aged 15+ years		
	Never	*Past*	*Present*	*Never*	*Past*	*Present*
	%	%	%	%	%	%
Ga						
Total	22	2	76	55	37	8
Male	12	2	85	28	59	10
Female	28	2	70	72	23	6
Non-Ga						
Total	40	3	57	56	39	5
Male	24	2	74	49	45	6
Female	49	4	47	70	26	4

account for the imbalance in the age profiles and variations in demographic mobility between the sexes in the Ga census data.[25] Similarly, it may be that whereas non-Ga males migrate to the city irrespective of their preparation for effective participation in an industrial economy, selective factors govern the migration of women in such a way that only those who can participate in an industrial economy migrate to the city. This explanation accounts not only for the educational and sexual imbalances in the non-Ga data, but for variations in the educational data for non-Ga and Ga women. The validity of these inferences, of course, can be determined only by further research in Central Accra.

In summary, the contemporary Ga population of Central Accra represents a stable community of manual labourers, traders, and marginal élites. While the origins of this community antedate European contact, its growth and socio-economic attributes derive from historical processes associated with interaction between Ga and Western societies. In certain respects, the Central Accra Ga community constitutes a residual population insofar as more affluent and technologically skilled Ga have moved away to the new suburbs ringing the city. The continuity and stability of the Ga population and the orientation of its socio-economic structure toward less skilled western occupational categories provide the sociological preconditions for the maintenance of aspects of the traditional social system which are not directly associated with the modern industrial urban complex. In subsequent chapters, I consider both the continuing relevance and the modification of traditional kinship standards within the Ga community of Central Accra.

REFERENCES

1. J. M. Bruce-Myers, 'The Origin of the Gas', *Journal of the African Society* 27, 1927–8, p. 168; A. B. Quartey-Papafio, 'The Native Tribunals of the Akras of the Gold Coast', *Journal of the African Society 10*, 1911, p. 320.

2. Paul Ozanne, 'Notes on the Early Historic Archaeology of Accra', *Transactions of the Historical Society of Ghana*' 6, 1962, p. 66.

3. The site of Great Accra has been identified as 'Ayaso, eleven miles northeast of Accra ($5°40'$ N; $0°18'$ W). Here middens mark the site of a large town extending for a mile along the southern bank of the small River Nsachi, and across the stream to the modern village of Amanfro' (Ozanne: 52). The dating of European ceramics at Ayawaso indicates that the town was founded at the turn of the seventeenth century (ibid.: 69) which suggests that the site of Great Accra may have changed during the early historic period.

4. Paul Ozanne, 'Notes on the Later Prehistory of Accra', *Journal of the Historical Society of Nigeria 3*, 1964, p. 20; Ozanne 1962: 67.

5. Ozanne 1962: 64—5.

6. Ozanne 1964: 20.

7. Ivor Wilks, 'Some Glimpses into the Early History of Accra', (MS), p. 6.

8. Ivor Wilks, 'The Rise of the Akwamu Empire, 1650—1710', *Transactions of the Historical Society of Ghana 3*, 1957, p. 104.

9. ibid.: 107.

10. ibid.: 105, 108.

11. Wilks (MS), p. 10.

12. E. A. Boateng, 'The Growth and Functions of Accra', *Bulletin of the Ghana Geographical Association 4*, 1959, p. 4.

13. Ioné Acquah, *Accra Survey*, London, 1958, p. 17.

14. William A. Hance, *Population, Migration, and Urbanization in Africa*, New York, 1970, pp. 330—1.

15. Acquah: 21; cf. Kwamina B. Dickson, *A Historical Geography of Ghana*, Cambridge, 1969, pp. 258—9.

16. See Boateng, p. 6.

17. Acquah: 28.

18. Frank E. K. Amoah, 'Accra: A Study of the Development of a West African City', (MS, 1964), pp. 81—2.

19. C. W. Armstrong, 'A Journal of a Century Ago', *The Teachers' Journal 9*, 1937, p. 7.

20. Government Documents 1891:42; 1902:20; 1911:19; 1923:50; 1932:79; 1950:26; 1964:3. In 1970 the population of a more territorially restricted Accra had mushroomed to 564,194 (Government Document 1972:202—3).

21. The demographic data presented in this chapter are based on the 1960 Ghana census. This census, which was supervised by the United Nations, is the most detailed census for any sub-Saharan African country. Among the volumes issued in the spring of 1965 are *Statistics of Towns* and *Tribes in Ghana*. Unfortunately neither volume contains information included in the other; consequently, the ethnic composition of particular urban units is not available from the published data. Shortly before I left Ghana, I was given access to the raw census data on Central Accra. From these census schedules, information on Ga living within Central Accra was obtained. By comparing the Ga figures for specific enumeration areas with those published in Part III of *Statistics of Towns* for the same areas, it is possible to draw a profile of the Ga and non-Ga populations in Central Accra for 1960. By comparing the Ga data for Central Accra with the information on the total Ga population published in *Tribes in Ghana* a similar profile can be drawn comparing the Central Accra Ga and the Ghana Ga populations. The statistics used in this discussion derive from these three sources. (Comparable data are not available for 1970 nor is a tribal volume projected for the 1970 census.)

22. In 1960, the total Ga population in Ghana numbered 235,210 or 3.5 per cent of the national population. The Central Accra Ga, therefore, represent 15 per cent of the Ghana Ga population.

23. e.g. Charles Newcomb, 'Graphic Presentation of Age and Sex Distribution of Population in the City', in P. K. Hatt and A. J. Reiss (eds.), *Cities and Society*, Chicago, 1959, pp. 382–92; Daniel F. McCall, 'Dynamics of Urbanization in Africa', in Simon and Phoebe Ottenberg (eds.), *Cultures and Societies of Africa*, New York, 1960, pp. 522–35. When population pyramids for the two populations are compared, the differences in the age and sex distributions of Ga and non-Ga populations are even more striking.

FIGURE 1
POPULATION PYRAMIDS FOR GA AND NON-GA, CENTRAL ACCRA, 1960

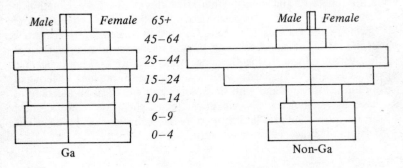

24. e.g. Astrid Nypan, 'Market Trade: A Sample Survey of Market Traders in Accra', *African Business Series, No. 2*, University College of Ghana, 1960.

25. Within the Central Accra Ga population, 95 per cent females and 88 per cent males were born in Accra.

CHAPTER II

GA CONCEPTIONS OF KINSHIP

If the longevity and demographic attributes of the Ga population in Central Accra produce a social matrix facilitating the perpetuation of aspects of the Ga kinship system, Ga kinship conceptions constitute a second set of prerequisites for an analysis of the empirical operations of the system.[1] In analysing Ga conceptions of kinship, I am concerned primarily with consistencies and inconsistencies in the ideal ordering of kinship institutions and with the sources and empirical implications of these inconsistencies. My analytical focus, therefore, concerns how certain ideas impose limits upon social behaviour and also allow freedom of choice within these limits.

Physiological Conceptions

The principles of Ga kinship rest upon concepts associated with three physiological phenomena or processes: blood, sex, and age. Concepts of blood are relevant to an understanding of the descent system and are essential in establishing a person's identity within certain social groups; these social units, in turn, determine his rights to certain forms of property and place limits on the contracts which he may make during his life. Concepts concerning age are pertinent to an understanding of jural authority within social groups, the distribution of usufruct rights to property owned by these groups, and the establishment of contracts between groups. Ideas about the sexes and their relations are essential for an appreciation of both the ordering of social units and authority within these groups, and the distribution of and accession to property. The domain of each of these fundamental sets of ideas, therefore, overlaps the domains of the others in certain respects, and it is this overlapping of spheres of interest which leads to conflicts and inconsistencies within the kinship system at the level of ideas as well as in practice.

In Ga society, blood (la) is a very potent social symbol with such complex and contradictory associations as life and death, war and chieftaincy, ritual purity and impurity, indissoluble bonds between human beings, and physical appearance. Two basic conceptions of blood as a substance are relevant to Ga kinship: the notion of blood as a quantitative substance, and the idea of blood in terms of density. Both concepts establish important aspects of a person's identity within Ga society.

The quantitative aspect of blood is essential for an understanding of cognatic descent in Ga society. Ga say that a person is related by blood to each of his grandparents and through them to their kin. When Ga speak of blood kinship, they conceptualize blood as a quantitative substance passing from generation to generation. It is appropriate to refer to kinsmen of the same or descendant generations as 'my blood (*mi la*)', but not to members of ascendant generations, for the blood of preceding generations flows into the veins of succeeding generations, while the converse is impossible.

Although an individual is related by blood to paternal and maternal grandparents, Ga believe that the greater proportion of blood is derived patrilineally. This conception is consistent with various other Ga ideas concerning social identity such as patronymy and tribal identity, for the child of an intertribal marriage belongs to the tribe of his father. Moreover, blood in its quantitative aspect is also related to certain ideas which Ga have concerning the relative importance of different kinship affiliations. Ga tend to emphasise their patrilineal ties when they discuss their social system abstractly or contrast it with the matrilineal systems of neighboring Akan-speaking peoples.

Apart from the quantitative conception of blood involving ideas about descent, the concept of blood in terms of density is related to physiognomy. A child resembles the parent whose blood is 'thickest'. A man may say that although his children have more of his blood, they resemble his wife, because her blood is thicker than his. Physical resemblance is an important social consideration. When a baby is born, women from the father's family are sent to examine the infant and make sure that its head, fingers, and toes resemble those of its mother or her husband. Although the child of a married woman is reckoned as her husband's offspring, adultery is one ground for divorce and entails financial compensation even if it does not lead to divorce.

A second major cluster of concepts surrounds age. Seniority in years is associated with seniority in social status. As a person ages, he assumes authority in the various social groups to which he belongs. The achievement of full social maturity is a life-long process for both men and women in Ga society.

In the case of a youth, the first stage in social maturation is achieved at physiological maturity. At that time his father presents him with a gun, a symbol of manhood in Ga society conveying the association of

manhood with the status of warrior. Not until a man marries does he
become semi-autonomous economically. Until that time he and his
father constitute an economic unit; any money which a youth may
receive should be given to his father who is responsible for defraying
the son's expenses. After marriage a man remains a jural minor until all
members of antecedent generations and those of his own generation
who are senior in age are dead.

In theory, therefore, a man's sphere of authority gradually expands
within ever-larger social units as senior members die. He first assumes
authority within his family of procreation; then after his father's death
among his siblings, and later within his family and kindred. This orderly
progression of increasing spheres of influence is mediated by certain
intervening factors, such as premature death and the process of
election. The senior members of different social units select their heads.
In this selection process considerations of personal ability may override
those associated with seniority in years. Theoretically, however,
seniority in age confers seniority in social status.

Certain of these processes are expressed in the succession to
headship in *Taki Kǫme we*, a branch of the Ga dynasty. This branch
has three subunits among which the office should rotate. During the
past seventy years, however, the office has been held by five
members of the same subunit: a fact which the present incumbent,
V, attributes to the marriages between the subunits in his father's
generation (see, A and II, B and I). When headman II died, it was

FIGURE 2
SUCCESSION TO HEADSHIP IN TAKI KǪME WE

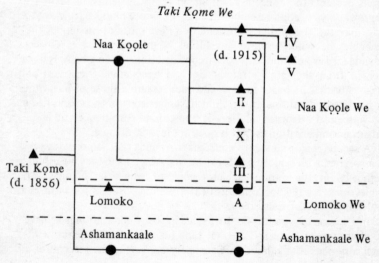

Taki Kǫme We

expected that his younger brother, X, would succeed him. The elders, however, selected his half-brother, III, in preference to X. The present incumbent, V, who is the only living male among his uterine siblings, anticipates that a nonuterine junior sibling will succeed him before the office passes to another subunit with *Taki Kome we*.

The third set of concepts on which the kinship system rests is associated with sex. The separation of the sexes has structural implications at all levels of Ga society. Every social group of males is complemented by a jurally autonomous group of females. Within families, therefore, councils of men supervise the conduct and affairs of male members, while complementary councils of women have authority over female members. Accession to property and distribution of property depend in large part upon sexual differentiations. Men acquire property from men, women from women. For this reason Ga people tend to emphasise the importance of patrilateral kin ties for men and matrilateral kin ties for women. Moreover, men and women live in separate dwelling groups: men with patrilaterally related kinsmen, women with matrilaterally related kinswomen. Formerly, the residential separation of the sexes was attributed to mystical sanctions, for menstruating women were believed to contaminate sacred objects in men's compounds. Thus in Ga society a major social principle is the separation of the sexes, with jural authority over each sex in the hands of members of the same sex.

From the viewpoint of the total society, however, women are subordinate to men. While women have independent authority within their own groups, they are jural minors within the total society. The subordination of females to males is expressed in many ways. Women are called 'left-handed people (*abekuloi*)', because they do things zigzaggedly (*dzabedzabe*), they cannot think clearly (*ame dzwenymo see*), or they are deceitful (*lakaloi*).[2] The seven days of the week are divided into four male days (*nuugbi*) and three female days (*yoogbi*); this differentiation has ritual significance, for ceremonies associated with marriage and death may be performed only on female days which are Monday, Thursday, and Saturday. Paternal kin are superordinate to maternal kin. When an infant is named, relatives symbolically receive it into the father's family by placing their hands on their right shoulders and then into the mother's family by placing their hands on their left shoulders. Although within families complementary councils of men and women govern the affairs of their own sex, the men's council has authority over the concerns of the family as a unit. When matters of general interest to the family are discussed, the male council may invite the female council to participate. Thus, the independent authority of each sex is modified by the ultimate authority of men in Ga society.

Social Institutions

These fundamental concepts associated with blood, age, and sex embody the principles on which Ga kinship structure rests. Certain ideas in each set are manifested in Ga concepts concerning descent, inheritance, marriage, and residence. These sets of physiologically based concepts, therefore, are necessary for an understanding of Ga social institutions.

The concept of blood as a quantitative substance is basic to an understanding of Ga descent. As I have mentioned, a person derives his blood from both parents, but a larger proportion comes from his father than his mother. Through his parents a person is related by indissoluble bonds of blood kinship to a virtually unlimited number of people. In practice, a person's effective kinship ties are with his grandparents' descendants, particularly his parents' and his own full siblings. Probably it is for this reason that Ga say that a person 'belongs to four relatives': his father's father, mother's father, mother's mother, and father's mother. Descent in Ga society, therefore, is cognatic, with emphasis on patrilineal affiliation.[3]

Structurally a cognatic descent system is more flexible and diffuse than one based on lineal principles. Within such a system, an individual probably has greater opportunity to emphasize those ties which appear beneficial to his interests. Not only are there no clearly defined limits, but the network of relations is the same for only full siblings. Nevertheless, Ga conceptualize three social units of increasing magnitude based on cognatic descent: *shia*, *we*, and *weku*.

As a social unit, *shia* (literally, house or building) refers to three generations of cognates or the cognatic descendants of a particular grandparent. *Shiai* are not stable groups, they are specific to particular individuals in particular social contexts. The composition of an individual's *shia* varies according to social situation and to his status in the life cycle. At any given time, however, a person's *shia* incorporates his closest living cognates, his 'immediate family'.

The next largest descent unit is *we* or family. Although Ga conceptualize a *we* as a branching tree, they can rarely trace their ancestry to the founder and do not bother to do so. While the founder of a *we* is usually a man, this is not always the case; as we have seen, two of the three branches of *Taki Kọme we* were founded by women.[4] *We* are corporate groups: every *we* has a name, an estate which includes land and titles to office, two sets of names which rotate between generations for the offspring of male members differentiating full siblings by sex and birth order, and often responsibility for the cult of a god who mediates relations between family members and the supreme being. Although membership in a *we* depends upon cognatic descent,

Ga emphasise their patrilineal affiliations. If a Ga is asked the name of his *we*, he first gives the name of his father's father's *we*; he may continue to name the *we* of his other grandparents. Yet cognatic descent rather than simply patrilineal descent entitles a person to share in the estate of the *we*.

Finally, the *weku* (*we*, family and *ku*, group) or kindred is sometimes used as a synonym for *we* but usually has a wider reference and pertains to all the blood relatives of an individual. *Wekunyo* means blood relative and all of a person's blood kinsmen are his *wekumẹi*. To differentiate between paternal and maternal kinsmen, Ga use the terms 'father's side (*tsẹsẹẹ*; literally, father's back)' and 'mother's side (*nyẹsẹẹ*)'. Each Ga person is considered to be related to four families through his grandparents. These distinctions were expressed by the spokeswoman for the bride's parents at one betrothal ceremony: 'Eight relatives are united; four relatives come from the woman's side and four relatives come from the man's side; all are joined in marriage (*wekumẹi kpaanyo efee ekome; wekumẹi edzwẹ dzẹ yoosẹẹ kẹ wekumẹi edzwẹ dzẹ nuusẹẹ yẹ gblaa mli*)'. *Weku* may be translated as kindred; the composition of which is similar only for offspring of the same parents.[5]

Consistent with a cognatic system of descent is the kinship terminology in which blood relatives are differentiated by generation and sex (see Table II/1).[6] Further differentiation within generations

TABLE II/1
REFERENCE TERMINOLOGY FOR KINSMEN*

Generation	Male Term	Bisexual Term	Female Term
5		*Nana-kọkrọ*	
4		*Nana-tshishiu*	
3		*Nana-kansua*	
2	*Nii*	—	*Naa*
1	*Tsẹ*	—	*Nyẹ*
Ego	*Nyẹmi-nuu*	*Nyẹmi*	*Nyẹmi-yoo*
1	*Bi-nuu*	*Bi*	*Bi-yoo*
2		*Nabi*	
3		*Nana-kansua*	
4		*Nana-tshishiu*	
5		*Nana-kọkrọ*	

*This terminology refers to blood kinsmen. Affinal terms are described in Table II/2. Any cognate can be classified according to this system. Thus, *Nii* incorporates FF, FFB, FFFBS, MF, MFB, etc; *Binuu* includes S, BS, ZS, MSS, MZDS, FBSS, FZSS, etc.

may be expressed by the following suffixes: *-onukpa* or elder, *-teng* or medial, and *-fio* or junior. Thus, one may refer to one's eldest sister as *nyẹmiyoo onukpa* or one's father's elder brother as *tsẹnukpa*. The significance of the reference terminology should not be overrated. While it is consistent with a cognatic descent system, a number of West African societies with unilineal descent systems have a similar kinship terminology.[7] Ga kinship terminology, therefore, provides supportive rather than conclusive evidence of cognatic descent in Ga society.

The basic conceptions of Ga descent, therefore, derive primarily from ideas associated with blood, and secondarily from ideas concerning the superordination of males. Jural authority within descent groups depends upon ideas associated with age, which I discuss in connection with institutions of inheritance and residence.

Concepts connected with blood, age, and sex determine accession to property. Accession to property depends first upon blood kinship and seniority and secondarily upon sex. Certain kinds of property such as lands, buildings, and titles form the estate of a family (*we*). Usufruct rights to such properties are distributed among the members of a family according to generational seniority and birth order. At the death of a holder of usufruct rights, the property reverts to the family for reallocation. If a man has usufruct rights to land belonging to his mother's father's family, after his death the family council meets to redistribute these land rights to another member of the family. In such redistributions the relative seniority of family members wishing to acquire these rights is a crucial consideration.

During a person's lifetime, he may acquire personal property such as land, buildings, money, and other forms of moveable wealth. At his death, the trustee of these properties is either a sibling of the same sex or, failing living siblings, the eldest child of the same sex. The trustee distributes the deceased's property among cognates in accordance with principles of seniority and sex. Thus while a man's acquired property may be distributed among his siblings and children (*bii*, who include his siblings' offspring), priority is given to his senior son (i.e., the eldest son of his senior wife). In a very real sense a man's senior son is heir to his social personality, for he becomes the spokesman for his father's children within the family (*we*) and as his father's generation dies assumes an increasingly authoritative voice within the family council. The special role of the senior son is reflected in the fact that it is he who receives his father's gun and usufruct rights to his father's room. Similarly, a woman's acquired property is distributed among her siblings and children, but her principal heir is her senior daughter. The sex of the original owner of a piece of property continues to be a relevant factor in subsequent transfers with particular consideration being given to descendants of the same sex. If a man acquires usufruct rights to land bought by his mother, his sister's daughters have first claim at his death. It is for this reason that certain Ga informants emphasize the importance of matrilateral kinship for females and patrilateral kinship for males; probably it also accounts for Quartey-Papafio's assertion that 'property which is tainted with female succession shall always be so'.[8]

While Ga initially emphasise patrilateral affiliation in discussing rights to property, further investigation discloses that cognatic affiliation is the salient factor. The rules for succession to the Ga stool are based on cognatic principles which are expressed clearly in the following excerpts from the *verbatim* proceedings of the 1932 Government enquiry into a Ga stool dispute.

I

A. According to Ga custom the grandchildren of Ga Manche are eligible to the Stool as inheritors.

Q. Supposing the grandchild of the Ga Manche was a female?

A. In that case if the granddaughter had a son, such a son was eligible to the Stool.

Q. Supposing such a son of the granddaughter of the Ga Manche had a father of a different Quarter [i.e., other than Abola]?

A. Such son of the granddaughter of the Ga Manche had the right to inherit the Stool . . . both descendants of male and female members of the Ga stool have power over the question of the enstoolment of Ga Manche.[9]

II

Q. Can you tell me the son of a female who has ever inherited the Ga Manche Stool?

A. Yes.

Q. Who?

A. Ga Manche Tackie Tawiah from Gbese.

Q. Can you tell us the name of his parents from Gbese and how he became Ga Manche?

A. Teikotsuru begat Akyereko (female). Teikotsuru was from Abola . . . Akyereko married to a man at Gbese and bore Teiko the father of Tackie Tawia – Ga Manche.

Q. What was the name of the husband of Akyereko?

A. I can't remember that now. I have another illustration where the son of a female had succeeded to the Ga Manche Stool. Narh Ayokkor Adu the daughter of Ga Manche Amugi bore Ofoli Kpakpo . . . Ofoli Kpakpo became Ga Manche.[10]

The importance of cognatic affiliation is exemplified in the kinship affiliations of the members of the male council of elders of the Ga stool in 1965. The essential criterion for membership on the council is descent from an occupant of the stool. Eight of the twenty-five members are matrilaterally affiliated through either mother's mother or mother's father, seventeen are patrilaterally affiliated. Ten of the latter, however, are connected to the stool through father's father and seven through father's mother. Thus 60 per cent of the male elders are related to the stool through some woman. Moreover, a majority of the officers of the council are affiliated to the stool through women.[11]

In summary, accession to property depends on blood kinship, the relative seniority of cognates, and considerations associated with the sex of the owner and the heir. These principles operate in contemporary Accra, at times to the chagrin of individuals. The continuing relevance of cognatic rights to property is illustrated clearly in the following case.

> Several years after the death in 1915 of a wealthy Ga trader, the house which he had built in Accra was sold by his senior son. Later one of his sons by a junior wife redeemed the property with money, part of which he had earned and part of which he had borrowed from his mother's sister. This purchase was in large measure an act of filial piety. The junior son assumed residence in the building and invited several uterine siblings to live in the house. He rented various rooms in the house and used the income first to repay his maternal aunt and later for his own use. In 1954 his non-uterine brothers took him to court claiming that the house belonged to all his father's sons and that the junior brother owed them compensation for the remuneration he had received from rents. Being a man of extreme sensitivity and high moral standards, the junior brother immediately moved from the house to another which he owned in one of the Accra suburbs. The court decided that the paternal brothers' claim was valid and that the junior brother should compensate them for the money which he had received and should appoint a caretaker to supervise the collection and distribution of rents among all the living brothers.

To some extent traditional norms are being modified by the making of wills. Increasingly individuals draw up wills to ensure that their own children will benefit from the fruits of their labours. Not infrequently, Ga complain that one of their parents died without making a will and consequently all his property went to his siblings rather than to his children. Legal wills are effective in so far as they limit the application of traditional norms. If they violate them, there is considerable difficulty.

> Thus, a noted herbalist left his house to one of his wives who was barren. His sons by other wives continued to live in the house and exerted a great deal of pressure on the old lady to leave the house and to return to her own kinsmen. Although she continues to live in her husband's house, she is extremely unhappy about her insecure position.

Concepts associated with blood kinship and seniority are relevant to an understanding of marriage in Ga society. Marriage is an alliance establishing a relationship between unrelated families (*we*). At the same time, it is a contract between individuals which can be broken by divorce and also extended beyond the life-times of the first conjugal pair. Since marriage is an alliance between families, rather than between individuals, it is formally the concern of those who have authority within families. Thus the parents of the spouses establish, dissolve, and extend the contract.

In establishing a marriage, the initiative is taken by the parents of the groom, particularly his father. Usually a youth informs his mother that he wishes to marry a certain girl; the mother consults his father and together they decide whether or not it is an appropriate marriage. In contracting a marriage, the primary concern is the morality or reputation (*dzengba*) of the family and the secondary one is the character of the girl. Among the factors which may deter a marriage are a family's reputation for witchcraft, quarrelsomeness, immorality, and the presence of 'incurable' diseases such as insanity and leprosy. In the past, the virginity of the girl is said to have been a major consideration; today, many brides are pregnant. Certain informants rationalized premarital pregnancy by saying that if a bride were not pregnant, some jealous woman might make her barren. If the man's parents agree on the proposed match, they request the girl's hand in marriage from her parents. When both sets of families have agreed to establish the contract, a series of financial prestations are made by the groom's family to that of the bride.

Marriage confers certain rights and obligations on the spouses. For Ga the main object of marriage is the procreation of children. Marriage gives a man exclusive rights to the sexuality of a woman. A barren woman (*kene*) is regarded as an unnatural person and Ga say that barrenness is the worst affliction that a woman can suffer. Each spouse is supposed to respect the 'parents' (i.e., senior kin) of the other. This deference is symbolized by a woman's annual prestation of firewood to her mother-in-law at the Rite of Feasting (*Homowo*) and by a man's offer to pay for the coffins of his parents-in-law. Certain economic obligations are imposed on both spouses. A woman is expected to cook for her husband, who should give her enough money to buy food and to support his children. Failure to honour any of these obligations may lead to divorce, which is the formal concern of the senior members of the families who contracted the marriage.[1][2]

After the dissolution of a marriage by divorce, a man continues to be responsible for the maintenance of the offspring of the marriage. Should a man fail to honour this obligation, his former wife attempts to coerce him to do so through his senior kinsmen. Traditionally, she also could resort to the Divisional Chief's Court and today she may appeal to the Municipal Court. Many of the cases appearing before the Accra Municipal Court in James Town during 1956–7 concerned the maintenance of children. The following case transcriptions, which were recorded in Ga by one of the three members of the court, are illuminating, for they disclose the processes by which sanctions are imposed, and various ideas concerning the relations between kinsmen and affines, parents and children, and men and women in Ga society.

I

Plaintiff: Dedei Kwashi. I live at Accra and sell things at the market. I had two children with the defendant, Ayi Ansah fourteen, Ama nine. He does not look after the children, so I brought him here.

Defendant: Joseph Teko Kwatia Hammond, farmer. We had two children. I had another wife. We quarrelled and the marriage was spoiled. I moved to Kumasi in 1950 and my wife did not come to say goodbye at the station, so I did not mind her. My mother wrote that the plaintiff was asking her for money. I replied that she should not heed her until she wrote herself. A letter came that Ama, one of the children, was sick. I sent £3 so that my wife could look after her. I wrote to my wife to come, but she did not answer.

Court: Defendant was told to give £5 every month for the children.

II

Plaintiff: Amaakai Anum, baker, Bubiashi. The defendant and I have three children: Oko [male], Daakua [female], and Oyoo [female]. When I was discharged from Korle Bu [hospital] a month ago, he said that he would take Daakua; I pleaded with him to let her stay as she is the one I send on errands. Before their father came for them, Daakua and Oko were with me for six years, their father did not look after them. Oko goes to school at Labadi where I visited him; when I told him to come to me during the holidays, he did not come. Daakua ran away from her father and came to me shortly before I was admitted to Korle Bu, at which time she returned to her father. When I was discharged, she refused to remain with her father, who said that he would bring Oko to me too. But I refused, I told him that a man looks after boys and a woman looks after girls, so he must take Oko.

After we went to sleep, Oko became ill. I took him to my brother, Anum, at the Post Office. My brother hired a taxi and we went to Labadi. The father was not in, but we saw his father's brother, Adziman. Adziman said he does not have a child called Oko, so we took the child to a herbalist at Mamprobi. Oko was having convulsions, he was given medicine. I told my brother Anum to take Oko. Anum said the father had come for the girl and so Oko was not his child, but if the father brought Daakua to him then he would take Oko also. Anum swore on 2s. drink that he would take both children and he said that the herbalist said he would cure Oko.

I stayed with Oko at the herbalist's in Mamprobi for two months and two weeks. Nobody came to visit us, because of the father. My husband said I should take the children and go to the herbalist and he paid £4. Then I took the children to my brother Anum and he said I must take them; I took them to Ataa Adziman who sent one of his sons to show me where the father lives. I told Ataa Adziman that I would visit them.

In a few days Oko came and said that his father had thrown him out. I told him to return. Before long he came again, and I took him back. Four months later Oko came again. He said his father had beaten him almost to death. I went and told my uncle who said that I must go and ask the father himself. I took him again to his father. He returned again. That is why I have brought the defendant.

Defendant: The plaintiff is my wife. We were divorced about twelve years ago. Nine years ago I went for the children. Eight years ago Daakua was sick; her mother did not come and I took her to a village where a herbalist cured her after seven months. I gave all the children to my mother to care for them. Six years ago I put Oko in the R. C. school. He became ill and came home; I took him to a herbalist in Kaneshi. When he ate plantains and groundnuts which he had been told not to eat, I beat him. I sent Daakua to go and catch him, but she refused . . .

Court: Plaintiff agrees to defendant's taking Oko, but Oko wants to stay with the plaintiff. The court said that since Oko is not well, he must live with the plaintiff, but the defendant must give £2 for the interval since he left him with the plaintiff and £1 every month hereafter.

When a married person dies, the alliance may be reaffirmed by extending the marital contract. The living spouse may marry one of the deceased's junior full siblings. While it is customary to make a formal acknowledgment of such a relationship, if the couple does not cohabit, the woman is free to marry another man. If a woman, however, marries a junior brother of her dead husband, their children are reckoned as the children of the deceased brother, which is symbolized by the continuation of the naming system. When a woman dies, her sister's children by the same man are not considered to be the offspring of the dead woman.

The marriage contract is intended to unite unrelated families. This belief imposes certain limits within which a person should not marry. A person should marry neither a cognate nor a cognate's spouse's cognate. In other words, an individual may marry neither a blood kinsman nor an affine's blood kinsman. In practice, if the kinship ties are remote, marriages may be established; one informant and his FFBSS (brother, *nyɛminuu*) married full sisters, and he commented 'it is wrong, but nobody said anything'.

There is one sanctioned exception to the rule forbidding marriage between cognates. This is cross-cousin marriage which is called 'immediate family marriage (*shiagblaa*)'. Although cross-cousin marriage is permitted with either cousin, Ga say that matrilateral cross-cousin marriage occurs more frequently. In fact, thirteen (52 per cent) of the twenty-five cross-cousin marriages on which data are available are between a man and his patrilateral cross-cousin. Cross-cousin marriage is considered to be a means of perpetuating close ties within families and of limiting the range within which property — especially titles to office — may be distributed. Certain informants said that it is a difficult relationship, because the roles of spouse and cognate may conflict and one can never 'get rid of the woman', because one is linked by indissoluble blood kinship bonds.

Polygyny is permitted and statistically fairly frequent in Ga society.[13] The first marriage of a man involves greater ritual and expense than subsequent ones, as is reflected in the terminology used to differentiate senior and junior wives. The former is called 'wedded woman (*kpeemǫyoo*)' and the latter is termed 'taken woman (*yoongǫ*)'. If the wives of a man are amicable, the junior ones refer to the senior one as 'mother (*nyę*)'; Ga informants have attributed the success of polygynous unions to the tact of their senior wives. Ga articulate the frictions inherent in polygynous unions; they speak of sexual jealousy and the concern of each wife for the welfare of her own children. In order to minimize such problems; a husband is expected to spend an equal amount of time with each wife in rotation. The ascribed period may be one week, two weeks, or longer. The wife who shares a man's bed is the one who prepares his food. Should another wife wish to discuss some issue with her husband, she may visit him for that purpose.

A number of terms differentiate categories of children. A full sibling is *fǫlǫ* and a paternal sibling is *musafin* (literally, half-belly). Although there is no single term to distinguish uterine siblings with different fathers, one can say 'he and I come from the mother's side (*mi kę lę dzę nyęsęę*)'. A wife's child by another marriage is termed *bamina*. Children of full siblings are also distinguished: *hiienyǫbii* are children of two brothers, *yeienyǫbii* are children of two sisters, and *nuubii kę yoobii* are children of a man and his sister.

Not only is there no single term for affines, but there are two categories of affines: those of kinsmen of ego's own and descendent generations and those of kinsmen of ascendant generations. The latter are referred to by the same terms as those for blood kinsmen, though they can be differentiated from them by adding 'by marriage (*yę gblaa gbę*)' to the basic term.[14] Ga say that they are classified as kinsmen, because their offspring are blood relatives. Moreover, marriage into the kindred of an ascendant affine is prohibited; for example, one may not marry into the kindred (*weku*) of ones FBW. While there is no collective term for affines of ego's own and descendent generations, they are referred to as 'male affines (*shaahii*)' and 'female affines (*shaayei*)'. The reference terminology for such affines is summarised in Table II/2. For a male ego, this system differentiates affines according to sex and a limited number of generations; for a female ego, according to generation and sex, except within her own generation. A woman refers to her brother's wife as wife (*nga*) and her husband's sister as husband (*wu*); Ga explain this usage by saying that siblings are one. The systems of affinal terminology emphasise and are consistent with cognatic descent.

Thus, since marriage in Ga society is an alliance uniting previously unrelated families, concepts pertaining to blood kinship and authority among kinsmen are of primary importance. Although marriage is an alliance which transfers limited rights in a woman to her husband's family, marriage is relatively stable. Nevertheless, in discussing conjugal relations an omnipresent notion is that since a marriage can be terminated by divorce, a person should be circumspect in the confidences which he exchanges with his spouse. Concerns which might be discussed freely with a kinsman ought not to be imparted to a spouse. As a marriage matures, a man and his wife may share mutual confidences as they would not have done earlier. In general, however, Ga are quite cynical about the trustworthiness of the opposite sex. Ga perceive the lives of men and women not only as different but as incompatible: a further manifestation of the basic antagonism between

TABLE II/2
REFERENCE TERMINOLOGY FOR AFFINES*

Male Ego				Female Ego			
Generation	Male	Female	Affinal Male	Male	Female	Affinal Female
2	Shaanii	Shaanaa	–	Shaanii	Shaanaa	–
1	Shaanuu	Shaayoo	–	Shaanuu	Shaayoo	–
Ego	Shabi	Nga	bentsima/ nikulafa	Wu	Wu/Nga	kulafa
1	Shaanuu	Shaayoo	–	Shaanuu	Shaayoo	–

*The following affines are included within various categories: *Shabi*: WB, ZH, FDH, FBDH[+]; *Nga*: W, BW, FBSW, WZ[+]; *Wu*: H, HB, HZ[+]; *Shaanuu*: WF, WFB, ZDH, DH, BDH; *Shaayoo*: BSW, SW, ZSW, WM, WMZ; *Shaanii*: WFF, WMF; *Shaanaa*: WMM, WFM; *Kulafa*: HBW; *Nikulafa*: WZH. (+: offspring of people in these categories are classified as children, *bii*) and radical separation of the sexes in Ga society. Throughout a person's life, his closest associations are with members of the same sex who are also blood kinsmen.

In discussing the residential system in Ga society, concepts associated with kinship, sex, and seniority are all relevant. The dichotomy between the sexes, however, is the basic consideration; in order to comprehend the structuring of dwelling groups, concepts pertaining to blood kinship and accession to property are also relevant. In traditional Ga society, men and women live in separate dwelling groups. Immature children live with their mothers, a youth begins to live in a male dwelling group when he is about ten years of age.

Although both men and women build houses in Ga society, traditionally the use of space in these buildings differs. A house built by a man is divided into two adjoining sections: one for men (*hiiashia*), one for women (*yẹiashia*); the house built by a woman consists only of a woman's section (*yẹiashia*). Within each section, the structural layout is similar: a number of rooms open onto a roofless compound. Not infrequently the buildings in Accra are two-storied, with the rooms on the second floor opening onto an enclosed passageway overlooking the inner compound.[15] While a number of women and children may share a room, each man occupies a single room. These spatial differences have implications for the structuring of dwelling groups within houses built by men and women.

It will be recalled that access to property depends first on blood kinship and secondly on sex. A man, therefore, tends to acquire property rights from patrilateral kinsmen, a woman from matrilateral kinswomen. These considerations explain the organization of dwelling groups in men's compounds and women's houses; they also partially account for the composition of dwelling groups in the women's compounds within men's houses. Thus, the men living in a compound are agnatic descendants of the builder; the women living in a building owned by a woman are matrilaterally related to the builder. Residential rules governing the occupancy of the women's section of a man's house are less precise. Daughters of the builder and wives of the men residing in the men's section are entitled to rooms within the women's compounds. In such compounds, cognatically affiliated women have life-long rights, while affinally affiliated women have limited rights. The latter may reside in the compound for the duration of their marriages; when their marriages are terminated either by death or divorce, they must return to live with their own cognates.

Houses are probably the most important form of property in Ga society. The social significance of building a house is far greater than the economic implications of converting moveable property into immoveable property or of deriving fluid capital from rents. It is a means of perpetuating one's identity within the otherwise highly fluid cognatic descent system. Ga acknowledge that a person who builds a house is likely to be remembered longer than one who does not, for the house is named after him, his children continue to live in it, and with the passing of generations it becomes an ancestral home for his descendants. Not only the building as a whole but the special usages attached to his room symbolize his continuing social identity. When his agnatic descendants die, they are 'laid in state' in this room. If the building is very large, his room may be reserved for such occasions; if it is relatively small, someone may live in the room except on such occasions. It is to this building that his agnatic descendants are brought for their naming rites and that his cognatic descendants return annually at the Rite of Feasting (*Homowo*) in which dead and living members of the family are believed to participate. Thus, physical structures serve as visible reminders of fixed points in an otherwise amorphous cognatic descent system.

Operation of the Social System

These social institutions and the principles on which they are based constitute an ideal system which has certain consistencies and in-consistencies. The consistencies within the system derive from the basic sets of ideas associated with the physiological categories of blood, age, and sex. The repetition of the same concept and/or related concepts from each of these sets of ideas leads to harmonious consistency within different institutions and provides the basis for linkages between institutions. The operation of the system at both the level of ideas and in practice depends, however, on inconsistencies which both give the system itself flexibility and provide individuals with opportunities of choice in confronting and using the system for their own benefit.

Within the ideal social system there are two main sources of inconsistency. The first type derives from the contradictory nature of ideas associated with each physiological category; the second results from differences in the weighting of ideas associated with different physiological categories in different institutions. The principles associ-ated with the same physiological category may conflict. Among the contradictory notions associated with sex are equality between the sexes and the superordination of males, with blood are cognatic descent and the emphasis on patrilineal descent, with age are the associa-tion of seniority in years with seniority in social status and the association of seniority in years with seniority in social status and the electoral process. Such contradictory concepts may be relevant in a single institution or in different institutions. The idea of equality between the sexes is relevant to an understanding of the structuring of descent groups, the ordering of dwelling groups, and accession to property. The superordinate status of males, on the other hand, pertains to the structure of authority within descent groups and to the institution of marriage. Similarly, cognatic descent is relevant to the ordering of social groups, kinship and affinal terminologies, and to an understanding of inheritance; patrilineal descent, however, is important in the naming system, the Ga view of their social system in contrast to those of other Ghanaian peoples, and the residential pattern. Conflicting notions associated with age and authority are relevant to an appreciation of the ordering of social groups and inheritance. While there are conflicting notions associated with each basic physiological category, one of these is considered to be primary and the others are secondary and, in a sense, alternatives to the first. With respect to blood, the central concept is cognatic descent; to age, it is the association of authority with seniority in years; and to sex, it is the superordinate status of males. Probably, the dominance of one concept in the cluster of concepts associated with physiological category facilitates the perception of a consistent social system by its participants.

Another type of inconsistency within the idealized social system is the dominance of different sets of ideas in different institutions. Concepts associated with blood are of primary importance in descent, marriage, and inheritance; those associated with age are dominant in considerations of authority within groups, and those pertaining to sex are paramount in the ordering of dwelling groups. While it is possible to analyse one cluster of concepts as the central set of ideas associated with a particular institution, a full understanding of each institution can be achieved only by considering concepts which derive from different sets. Moreover, the relative importance of different sets of ideas within particular institutions varies. The consideration of the dominant set by itself gives a more or less complete notion of particular institutions. Thus, while it is probably correct to state that inheritance involves primarily concepts associated with blood, concepts associated with age and sex are almost of equal significance. Whereas if one knows about concepts associated with blood in relation to descent, one understands a great deal more about the descent system *per se* without considering other types of concepts.

In the operation of the social system in practice, there are two main types of inconsistencies: intrinsic and extrinsic. The intrinsic factors are the type which I have been discussing: they constitute the strength of the system, for they give individuals an opportunity to choose between alternative possibilities in particular situations. Without such alternatives the system would probably be too rigid to operate effectively.

These alternatives provide limits within which individuals can make choices and still participate within the system. For example, a man should live with male agnates; it may be, however, that while there is no available space in the houses of close patrikinsmen, there is a vacant room in the house of his mother's brother. By emphasising cognatic affiliations rather than patrilineal ones, he may make use of his maternal uncle's room. Such a decision would be considered irregular, but not illegal. Thus intrinsic inconsistencies permit the social system to operate in practice and the idealized system to remain intact.

On the other hand, extrinsic inconsistencies have very different implications for the social system. This type of inconsistency derives from factors which are external to the social system. They are associated primarily with the modernization process in general and with Christianity, western education, and a money economy in particular. Although Ga have had intensive experience with western institutions within the last century, their social system has proved to be remarkably resilient. In part, this is due to the fact that extrinsic factors not only have led to obvious inconsistencies but have reinforced certain principles within the social system. For example, a very high proportion of Ga women with limited western education are traders; their economic independence may well intensify the institutional separation of the sexes in Ga society. Similarly, the greater access of males to western education and consequently to white collar jobs reinforces the principle of male superordination. Thus, while contact with western institutions has limited the application of certain traditional principles, it has emphasised others.

Nevertheless, Christianity, western education, and new occupational possibilities have led to new values and institutional modifications in Ga society. Christian ideals with respect to monogamous marriages and the consequent emphasis on the conjugal family have led to modifications in the range of kinship ties which is reflected in the making of wills and to a lesser extent in the residential pattern. The western educational system has introduced ideas of social status based on new occupational skills, which may conflict with principles of authority associated with age. A new associational concept resulting from the impact of an industrial economy is 'friendship'. This is a concept which is quite alien to older members of Ga society but which is important in the recreational life of young and middle-aged men and women. Bonds of friendship, rather than kinship, constitute the basis of voluntary associations, such as mutual aid societies and football clubs.[16] The structure of these associations is based on a combination of principles which may include friendship, locality, occupation, age, and sex; in any association one of these principles is perceived as central and the others as secondary. While such extrinsic factors impinge upon the operation of the traditional social system and offer certain alternatives to it, their overall effect has been considerably less than might be expected given the proportion of members of professional and white-collar occupational categories among the Ga in Central Accra. The relative stability of the social system in Central Accra is probably related to the continuity of the community over time with its obvious implications for the structuring of enduring social relations. At the same time, the impingement of extrinsic factors on the social system indicate social cleavages and alternative ideas which may be expected to be increasingly accentuated as participation in the modern sector broadens. The following chapters are concerned with an analysis of the empirical operation of Ga kinship conceptions with respect to the ordering of residential units and ceremonial networks in Central Accra.

REFERENCES

1. In a paper on kinship studies, Lévi-Strauss has maintained that 'logical priority' should be given to ideological rather than quantitative models, because of potential discrepancies and contradictions between the former model and 'its empirical applications'. (C. Lévi-Strauss, 'The Future of Kinship Studies', Proceedings of the Royal Anthropological Institute for 1965, 1965, p. 16). I would further argue that in ethnographic analysis the appropriate ideological models should be established first, because these models offer insights into the ordering of statistical data. When statistical models are considered in the light of indigenous ideological models, their interpretation is more likely to accord with the indigenous interpretation of these data. The ethnographer, therefore, is more likely to avoid the ethnocentrism which seems to me to be the basic fallacy inherent in contemporary 'componential analysis' in American cultural anthropology. A similar charge may be levelled against M. G. Smith's otherwise methodologically superb analysis of the derivation of structural principles in West Indian family structure from quantitative data alone (M. G. Smith, *West Indian Family Structure*, Seattle, 1962).

2. Both in the field and in correspondence, it has been impossible to elicit comparable phrases for men from Ga informants.

3. It should be noted that my classification of Ga descent differs from the influential interpretation of M. J. Field, whose pioneering studies in Ga ethnography were first published in 1937 and 1940. Field characterizes Ga descent as unequivocally patrilineal (M. J. Field, *Social Organisation of the Ga People*, London, 1940, pp. 1, 52n).

4. See p. 27.

5. In theory, social units are co-ordinate with territorial units. There are three categories of territorial units: *shia*, *kutsho*, and *mang*. *Shia* refers to a house built by an individual which bears his name. If the builder is also the founder of a family, the building may be referred to as *we* rather than *shia*. *Kutsho* refers to a major subdivision of a town

within which people are thought to be distantly related by blood, either because the original settlers were kinsmen or because of intermarriage. *Mang* refers to the entire area of a town, though it may be used to refer to the total Ga state.

Although Ga are primarily town dwellers, there are many villages within the Ga state. Each village is linked through its founder to a particular town family and through the family to a specific *kutsho*. Thus, a village court case could be sent for appeal from the court of the village headman to that of the chief of the *kutsho* and from that court to the court of the Ga paramount chief in Accra.

The following diagram expresses these territorial distinctions:

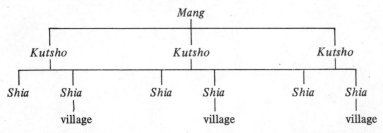

6. Terms of address are more variable. An individual calls females of the first ascendant generation *Awo* and males *Ataa*; members of second ascendant generations are called by the reference terms, *Nii* and *Naa*. Members of ones own and descendent generations are called by their personal names until they become parents, at which time a teknonymous name becomes appropriate such as *Adenyę* or *Adetsę*, which mean mother of *Ade* and father of *Ade*, respectively.

7. e.g. Yoruba.

8. A. B. Quartey-Papafio, 'Law of Succession among the Akras or the Ga Tribes Proper of the Gold Coast'. *Journal of the African Society 10*, 1910, p. 65. Another factor is that in certain parts of Accra where Akan immigrants have settled, MB-ZS inheritance is normative; see Ivor Wilks, 'Akwamu and Otublohum: An Eighteenth-Century Akan Marriage Arrangement'. *Africa*, 29, 1959, pp. 391–404.

9. Government Document 1932b: 135–6.

10. Government Document 1932b: 168.

11. The head of the council through his MM, three through FM, and three through FF.

12. Divorce is, however, relatively infrequent. Of the most recent marriages of 215 Ga women interviewed in Central Accra, 44 were widowed, 138 were married, and 33 were divorced. The divorce ratio is 19 per cent of all marriages which had not been terminated by death. These figures, however, only apply to the last marriages of these 215 women, because the data on previous marriages are not sufficiently reliable.

13. In Central Accra, 53 (38 per cent) of 138 current marriages of female informants are polygynous; 10 (13 per cent) of 78 current marriages of male informants are polygynous.

14. e.g., *Nii*: FF, MF: FMH, MMH; *Nyę*: M: MBW; FW, FBW; *Tsę*: F:MZH.

15. In Central Accra the larger buildings are constructed from *swish* (a wooden frame covered by mud), though there are also wooden and concrete houses; the smaller dwellings are made from either *swish* or corrugated iron.

16. Since the Ga are indigenous to Accra, ethnic affiliations have not constituted the basis for forming mutual aid societies, except for Ga who have migrated from other towns.

CHAPTER III

GA RESIDENCE IN CENTRAL ACCRA

From a consideration of aspects of the ideal kinship system of the Ga people, I now turn to the empirical operation of this system in the ordering of residential units in Central Accra. My discussion focuses upon the relations between Ga models of residence and statistical data on Ga households in Central Accra. The interpretation of these relations is necessarily complex in analysing a situation of social change where one must decide whether or not to attribute discrepancies between the ideological and statistical orders to the empirical operation of the traditional ideas or to factors associated with social change. M. G. Smith has stated this problem concisely: 'Structural differences express themselves in differing frequencies ... but frequency differences do not always represent or entail differences of structure'.[1] In general, Ga residential structure exhibits continuity at the level of structural principle and change at the level of the interconnection of these principles. It, therefore, appears that there has been less change in the Ga residential system than a cursory examination of quantitative data on contemporary residential units might suggest.

In order to interpret the structure of actual residential units, two Ga models of residential structure are relevant. These models are polar types, for one is the Ga model of the 'traditional' residential system and the other of the 'modern' system. As such, they constitute Ga conceptions of radical residential alternatives which any Ga might formulate, irrespective of his or her evaluation of their desirability. Both models are relevant to the understanding of the ordering of actual residential units.

As I have described, Ga say that traditionally men and women live in separate houses. Boys go to live in their fathers' houses at about ten years of age. While the physical residential separation of men and women is an inviolate principle of the traditional residential system, Ga say that three types of dwelling units exist whose occupants' relationship is determined by the sex of the genealogically senior member: (1) a men's house occupied by patrilaterally related men, (2) a women's house occupied by matrilaterally related women and their children, and (3) a house with a section for patrilaterally related men and an adjacent section for women who may be either patrilaterally affiliated to the male household or wives of men living in the men's compound. In the traditional model, therefore, the sex of the household head determines the relationship between the occupants of a dwelling. If the head is a man, occupants are patrilaterally related men and women or wives and children of these men; if the head is a woman, the occupants are matrilaterally related women and children. From this model, four structural principles for traditional Ga residence can be deduced: (1) the separation of adults of opposite sex, (2) the sex of the household head as the determinant of the members' affiliation and their age and sex distribution, (3) the authority of the geneaologically senior member, and (4) the superordination of males.

In order for such a residential system to work and for society to perpetuate itself, the various types of residential units can not be strictly autonomous, for the production of children must be assured. This is achieved through the allocation of space within dwellings. In Ga houses every man has his own room, while several women and their children may share a single room. When a man wishes to have sexual relations with his wife, he calls her to spend the night in his room. In a polygynous marriage, each wife in rotation has a prescribed interval during which it is her duty and right to sleep with her husband and to prepare his meals, which usually are prepared at the woman's house and brought by her or one of her children to the man's house. For a polygynous husband the interval of connubial service is the same for each wife. These procedures imply that the population of a dwelling fluctuates between day and night and from one night to another, and that while men sleep in their own houses, women may sleep elsewhere.

The Ga model for the modern residential unit contrasts radically with the traditional model which I have just described. The modern unit is the independent conjugal family composed of a man, his wife and their children. This model has developed in response to association with Western institutions. The extent to which the achievement of such a domestic unit is an aspiration within the contemporary Ga population probably varies with age and the socio-economic factors which limit its actual achievement. Nevertheless, the independent conjugal family model is based on two structural principles: (1) the co-residence of a married couple, and (2) the superordination of the husband. It is noteworthy that the principle of male superordination is relevant to both traditional and modern models of Ga residence, which necessarily complicates the interpretation of quantitative data.

Although Ga may have other models of their residential system, these polar types are sufficient for understanding the structuring of actual residential units and interpreting structural changes.

The quantitative data which I present were collected in standardized interviews with Ga living in Central Accra.[2] In analysing Ga residential units, I have followed Smith's maxim that 'the appropriate units (of study) are the total samples rather than their constituent households.'[3]

In Central Accra houses are rarely occupied by a single household, which I define as a co-resident group who consider themselves to constitute a co-residential unit and who are usually interrelated by cognatic and/or affinal ties.[4] On the basis of this definition, the sample comprises eighty households occupying fifty-six dwelling units in Central Accra.

According to the traditional Ga model of residential structure, the basic principle is the separation of adult men and women. This rule, however, pertains to only 36 per cent of the Accra households composed of two or more persons (see Table III/1). Although it may be argued that the separation of the sexes was never realized in traditional Ga society, comparative data from old Tema village suggest that in recent years this principle has been adhered to in isolated Ga towns. Before resettlement, 77 per cent of Tema residential units were unisexual, whereas after resettlement only 14 per cent were unisexual.[5] The discrepancy between the jural norm and the quantitative data for the Central Accra Ga can be explained with relative ease. It will be recalled that the traditional principle was backed by mystical sanctions which do not appear to be relevant for most Ga today.[6] The Tema data suggest, however, that although a belief may lose its potency, associated behavioural practices need not change unless situational factors change radically as in the Tema resettlement context. Although an explicit analogue to Tema resettlement does not exist for Central Accra, the result of the severe 1939 earthquake which partially or completely

TABLE III/1
CLASSIFICATION OF GA HOUSEHOLD
UNITS BY SEX OF HOUSEHOLD HEAD

Type of Household	Household Head	
	Male	Female
Single individual	5	8
Conjugal family	9	—
Bisexual kin unit	11	23
Unisexual kin unit	5	19
Total	30	50

destroyed many dwellings is comparable in some ways. When the houses were rebuilt, Ga say that they were not rebuilt in accordance with the traditional pattern of a men's compound and an adjacent women's compound, rather a single dwelling unit was constructed in which certain rooms were allocated for the use of men and others for the use of women.

Another major principle of the traditional Ga residential system is that the sex of the household head determines the affiliation of members in such a way that households under the authority of males will be patrilaterally affiliated and those under the authority of females will be matrilaterally affiliated. In post-1939 Central Accra, therefore, one would expect to find three types of household units: (1) unisexual units with female heads and matrilaterally affiliated members, (2) unisexual units with male heads and patrilaterally affiliated members, and (3) bisexual units with male heads and patrilaterally and affinally affiliated members. Nevertheless, the independent conjugal family unit is not appropriate to the modified traditional Ga residential model. If the widest latitude is given to the interpretation of affiliation rules by saying that it is appropriate in households with male heads to include all patrilateral relatives and affinally related women and that it is appropriate in households with female heads to include matrilaterally related females of all ages and males under fifteen years, a larger proportion of members of households with female heads are living appropriately than members of households with male heads (see Tables II/2 and II/3).

The sex of the household head is also relevant to the age and sex composition of the household. According to the strict interpretation of traditional residential rules, children under fifteen and adult women should live in units with female heads, whereas adult men should be found in units with male heads. As the data in Table X shows, the overwhelming proportion of women and children live in accordance with this norm, while the proportion of adult men living under the authority of women is approximately equal to those living under the authority of men. The explanation for this probably relates to the proportion of female heads in the sample (63 per cent). The large number of female household heads is due to the preponderance of women in the Ga population of Central Accra, which reflects not only the stability of the Ga community in Accra but certain differences in the socio-economic status of men and women.[7] As I have mentioned, men have had greater access than women to western education and thereby to the requisite skills for effective participation in the modern industrial economy. Whenever possible, individuals seek to invest in real estate and today, due to the scarcity of unoccupied land in Central Accra, buildings are constructed in adjacent suburbs. There is a

TABLE III/2
AFFILIATION TO HEAD, AGE AND SEX OF
HOUSEHOLD MEMBERS

Member	Household Head	
	Male	*Female*
Matrilateral	%	%
Male		
0−14	9	16
15+	6	9
Female		
0−14	9	34
15+	14	25
Patrilateral		
Male		
0−14	13	21
15+	21	1
Female		
0−14	14	3
15+	5	2
Affinal		
Male		
0−14	0	*
15+	*	2
Female		
0−14	0	2
15+	8	3
Total %	99	99
N.	224	510

*under 0.5 per cent.

tendency, therefore, for financially successful individuals, who are usually men, to move out of Central Accra, leaving behind a less well-educated, less affluent, predominantly female population.[8] A consideration of the sex distribution of household heads does not show a significant difference between men and women, which suggests that men and women are equally likely to become household heads in Central Accra.[9]

A third major principle of Ga traditional residence is that the household head is the genealogically senior person in the unit. This rule applies in every kin-based residential unit in the sample with one exception. The single exception is a sixty-year-old man who is the head of a household composed primarily of matrilateral kinswomen. In this case, the principle of male superordination operates, probably because

TABLE III/3
SUMMARY: AGE, SEX, AND APPROPRIATENESS OF MEMBERS' RESIDENCE BY SEX OF HOUSEHOLD HEAD

Household Head	Male Members		Female Members[1]		Residence Appropriate[2]	
	0–14	*15+*	*0–14*	*15+*	*No*	*Yes*
	%	%	%	%	%	%
Male	34	49	21	28	40	27
Female	66	51	79	72	60	73
Total %	100	100	100	100	100	100
N	141	127	252	214	211	523

1. $X^2 = 6.03; P < .025$
2. $X^2 = 13.9; P < .001.$

of the man's chronological age, but the affiliation of the members of his household relates to kinship with the builder of the house rather than with the current head. This case, therefore, raises another important issue, accession to headship and its relation to the composition of residential units.

An individual becomes head of a household either by establishing an independent unit or by succeeding to the position. An independent unit may be established either by building a house or by renting space in a house. The variant modes of assuming authority have implications for the continuity of the household over time, which is reflected in the size and generational depth of household units. Although there is a high proportion of tenant households in Central Accra, the majority of senior members of both sexes have succeeded to the position formerly held by a kinsman.[10] As I have noted, accession to all forms of property depends on cognatic affiliation and sex.[11] At the death of a male house-builder, a patrikinsman should succeed him; whereas at the death of a female house-builder, a matrikinswoman should succeed her. The data in Table III/4 suggest that men adhere more closely to traditional rules of succession than women. The greater variability in the mode of succession for women probably relates to the greater ability of men to realize their ambition of building houses which facilitate the perpetuation of their social identity within an otherwise fluid cognatic descent system. Since houses must be built outside Central Accra, the 'family' houses in Central Accra are left for the use of poorer female relatives who accede to headship by emphasising cognatic affiliations and disregarding the sex of their predecessors.

As a final comment on accession to headship, it should be noted that while members of both sexes have succeeded matrikinswomen, no one has succeeded a patrikinswoman. Such a mode of accession to headship

TABLE III/4
RELATIONSHIP OF HOUSEHOLD HEAD TO
BUILDER

Relationship to Builder	Household Head	
	Male	Female
Single individual	14	19
Patrilateral male	12	8
Matrilateral male	2	7
Matrilateral female	2	12
Affinal male	0	4
N.	30	50

for men does not violate the principle of sexual separation any more than succeeding a matrikinswoman; analogously, for women it violates the principle of matrilateral accession no more than does succeeding a patrikinsman. The non-occurrence of succession to a patrikinswoman probably relates to the residential rule for children who are expected to live with their mothers and, therefore, usually with their matrikins-women. People are never required to live with patrikinswomen; when they do, these women are subordinate members of a household headed by a patrilateral male. Probably the two instances in which men succeeded matrikinswomen can be explained by their lifelong member-ship in the household, whereas the succession of women to kinsmen can be explained by the socio-economic considerations which I have discussed.

As I have noted, with one exception the heads of kin-based residential units are the genealogically senior members, who are also invariably chronologically senior in age. A consideration of the age of the household head is relevant to the size and generational depth of residential units. Differences in the size and generational depth of units under male and female heads are shown in Table III/5. In general women are heads of larger residential units of greater generational depth than men. These differences may be attributed to the larger proportion of women who have succeeded to positions of authority in the Central Accra households.

The final principle of importance in both the traditional and the modern residential models is the superordination of males. This principle is relevant to an understanding of actual residential units in a number of ways. First, the principle of male superordination explains the matrilateral structure of units with female heads as shown in Table III/6. Since a man of the same generation and age as the female

TABLE III/5
SIZE AND GENERATIONAL DEPTH OF RESIDENTIAL UNITS BY
AGE AND SEX OF HOUSEHOLD HEAD

Household Head	*Size*				*Generation Depth*			
	1	*2–8*	*9–15*	*16+*	*1*	*2*	*3*	*4*
Male								
Under 45	4	2	0	0	4	8	0	0
45+	1	12	6	5	1	6	6	5
Female								
Under 45	1	8	0	0	1	6	2	0
45+	2	15	15	9	2	3	22	14
N.	8	37	21	14	8	23	30	19

household head would be unwilling to live under her authority, it may be inferred that women who have succeeded patrikinsmen as household heads have done so in default of suitable male successors. Although the core of such a household would be the woman's offspring and her uterine sisters and their children, a few patrilateral kinswomen might be included; the predominant principle of affiliation between the head and the members of the unit would be matrilateral. Thus, irrespective of the mode of accession to headship by women, household members are related to the head matrilaterally.

Secondly, the principle of male superordination accounts for the correspondence between affiliation to the builder and affiliation of members under male heads. Occasionally, men succeed matrikin as heads of residential units. When they succeed matrikinsmen, it is probably in default of appropriate patrilateral male heirs; given the principle of male superordination, their residence in the house need not imply the dispossession of any member of either sex to whom the new household heads are linked by matrilateral kinship ties. Succession to a matrikinswoman probably results from the men's lifelong residence in the household which violates the traditional residential rules but occurs in practice. At the death of the senior woman, such a man may become head of the unit by virtue of his sex even when generationally senior women live in the house.

Thirdly, the principle of male superordination is expressed in the proportion (11 per cent) of conjugal family units which relate to ideological and socio-economic changes accompanying the modernization process.

Turning to a consideration of the independent conjugal family as a model for residential structure, a variety of quantitative data is relevant.

TABLE III/6

AFFILIATION OF MEMBERS TO HOUSEHOLD HEADS BY HEAD'S
SEX AND RELATIONSHIP TO BUILDER

Affiliation of Members to Head	Head's Relationship to Builder						
	None		Patrilateral		Matrilateral		Affinal
	M.	F.	M.	F.	M.	F.	F.
Single individual	5	3	—	—	—	—	—
Conjugal family	5	—	1	—	—	—	—
Patrilateral	3	—	11	1	—	—	—
Matrilateral	1	16	—	7	4	19	3
Affinal	—	—	—	—	—	—	1
N	14	19	12	8	4	19	4

The conjugal family unit has been achieved in nine cases and in eighteen cases potentially independent conjugal units exist as dependent units within bisexual kin units. The eighteen dependent conjugal pairs are distributed among twelve bisexual kin units. In each case, the wife is living virilocally. While eight of the households with female heads have one dependent conjugal unit, the average for the four units with male heads is 2.5. Given the traditional rules which sanction the residence of wives in their husbands' houses, it is probable that a greater number of dependent conjugal units in households with female heads will evolve into independent nuclear family units than conjugal units in households with male heads.

Nevertheless, traditionally spouses should not live in the same compound and an analysis of the residence of 228 spouses of 216 Ga adults interviewed in Central Accra shows that this norm pertains to domestic organization in contemporary Accra. The data in Table III/7 show that membership in a monogamous marriage is the norm for both sexes, that with one exception conjugal co-residence is associated with monogamy, and that only 19 per cent of 139 monogamous unions are co-resident.[12] These data indicate that however salient the modern residential model may be, particularly in the aspirations of young clerks and teachers living in Central Accra, it is infrequently achieved in practice.

The statistical data on Ga households in Central Accra have implications not only for trends in the organization of actual household units but for the modification of the Ga conceptual model of their residential system. The data indicate that at present the dominant trend in household organization is away from unisexual kin units based on

TABLE III/7
FORM OF MARRIAGE AND RESIDENCE OF SPOUSE BY SEX OF
INFORMANT*

Residence of Spouse	Form of Marriage		
	Monogamous	Polygynous	
		2 wives	3 wives
Male Informants: Number	68	8	2
Same house	20	1	—
Central Accra	39	12	5
Elsewhere	9	3	1
Female Informants: Number	85	53	
Same house	20	1	
Central Accra	30	18	
Elsewhere	35	34	

*There are fourteen overlapping cases of males and females in the 'same house' category; intertribal marriages account for the remaining cases in this category.

unilateral affiliation towards bisexual kin units based on cognatic affiliation. Another trend is the emergence of the conjugal family as an independent residential unit. Both trends relate to socio-economic changes associated with the modernization process. More importantly, however, these data suggest that the Ga residential model has been modified not in terms of its constituent principles, but in the ordering of these principles.

In the traditional model, the basic principle of the residential system is the separation of the sexes, which has limited salience today.[13] Rather, the principle of male domination has superseded this notion and accounts for many of the variations expressed in the statistical data. Significantly, the modernization process has reinforced the principle of male superordination both ideologically and socio-economically. I suggest that the persistence of traditional residential principles at ideological and empirical levels is related to the socio-economic and demographic attributes of the Ga community in Central Accra, which I have discussed in Chapter I.

In conclusion, my analysis suggests the relevance of indigenous conceptual models for analysing quantitative residential data among the Ga in Central Accra. In interpreting the data, I have concentrated on the traditional residential model rather than on the modern residential model, in part because the conservative nature of the community dictated this choice, and in part because a genetic model seems most appropriate for attempting to understand social change. As Fortes has observed, 'growth is the product of two kinds of forces symbolized by the passage of time, those of continuity (conservative forces) and those of non-reversible modification'.[14] Although both types of forces are operative in contemporary Central Accra, the conservative forces hold sway over the forces for change at the level of residential structure in the Ga community of Central Accra.

REFERENCES

1. Smith 1962: 245.

2. The sample was based on the James Town Maternity Clinic social survey sample, which consisted of a 10 per cent random sample of all houses in Central Accra. From the Clinic sample, the first twenty houses in each of three sub-areas which included at least one Ga adult was chosen. Within each house, every Ga adult (over 15 years of age) was interviewed.

3. Smith 1962: 9.

4. Only 13 per cent of the houses in the sample were occupied by a single Ga household.

5. G. W. Amarteifio, D. A. P. Butcher, and D. Whitman, *Tema Manhean: A Study of Resettlement*, Accra, 1966, pp. 39—40.

6. In a standardized interview on Ga culture administered to 96 Ga household members in Accra (see Chapter V), only one individual explained the traditional residential separation of men and women as due to the polluting nature of women; moreover, this individual was living with his wife in a dwelling with his patrilateral kinsmen.

7. Females constitute 56 per cent of the total Ga population and 65 per cent of the Ga population over forty-five years of age.

8. See Chapter I and Acquah 1958: 32, 38.

9. 21 per cent males, 19 per cent females are household heads.

10. 45 per cent units with male heads and 33 per cent units with female heads are tenant households.

11. See Quartey-Papafio 1910—11, and A. N. Allott, 'A Note on the Ga Law of Succession'. *Bulletin of the School of Oriental and African Studies 15*, 1953, pp. 164—9.

12. 87 per cent men and 62 per cent women are married monogamously.

13. 30 per cent of the sample households are unisexual.

14. Fortes 1949: 55.

CHAPTER IV

CEREMONIES FOR GA
KINSMEN

Apart from the residential system, the most meaningful aspect of
kinship to the Ga inhabitants of Central Accra is the cycle of life crisis
ceremonies for kinsmen. These personal rites recur at irregular intervals
to mark similar biosocial transitions during the life span of each Ga
person.[1] The ceremonial groups which such *rites de passage* mobilize
are transitory groups based on cognatic and affinal ties with initiands.[2]
Consequently, life crisis ceremonies define and express minor kin units
and ramifying networks of personal association throughout the community.

In discussing the sociological implications of life crisis ceremonial, I
am concerned not with detailed analyses of the symbolism of particular
ceremonies, but with a consideration of the general social effects of
these rituals.[3] My discussion focuses first on the implications of the
traditional cycle of ceremonies for the social classification of persons
and for the ordering of ritual groups, and secondly on the effects of
new ideas arising from the modernization process upon the ceremonial
cycle. By modernization I refer to the process by which small-scale
societies are integrated into large-scale societies within the context of
western technological society. Although this definition has manifold
implications for the development and adaptation of ideas and institutions in 'developing' societies, my analysis is limited to a consideration
of several ideas resulting from social and economic changes and of the
relations between these ideas and Ga ritual. While the traditional cycle
of life crisis ceremonies continues to be performed in contemporary
Accra, it has been modified. As I attempt to show, life crisis ceremonies
have readily incorporated new ideas, and this, I believe, accounts for
the continuing relevance of this ceremonial system in contemporary
Central Accra.

The Traditional Ceremonial Cycle

The aim of the cycle of life crisis ceremonies, which is based on the physiological development of the human organism, is to mark status transitions during the human life span. Each successive ceremony introduces a further phase in the process of social maturation from infant to ancestor. Each ceremony defines an individual as a member of a bio-social category and failure to observe a ceremony entails mystical and practical sanctions. The ceremonial cycle, therefore, is a means of establishing bio-social categories and of ordering relations between such categories of human beings.

Ritual marks five major social transitions during the life span of every Ga person who lives to adulthood. The naming rite (*kpodziemọ*) transforms an eight-day-old infant from a biological organism into a Ga person. An infant who dies during the first week of life is not considered to be a social being and its mother does not achieve the respected status of motherhood reflected in the use of a teknonymous name. The naming ceremony which is performed for all infants born either to a married Ga man, that is to a man who had made marriage payments for the mother of the child, whether the mother be Ga or non-Ga, or to an unmarried Ga woman establishes the child's ethnic identity as a Ga and its membership of a particular kindred.

The circumcision ceremony (*hiianii*, men's things) which may be performed at any time between the naming ceremony and approximately ten years of age, establishes the masculine identity of boys (*efee nuu*, he is made a man). Although complete data on the meaning of the circumcision ceremony are not available, it appears that the male foreskin is likened to female genitalia and that the removal of the foreskin clarifies the ambivalent sexual identity of an uncircumcised male. The association of the foreskin with femininity is consistent with the belief that an uncircumcised male is ritually impure and would be barred from certain sacred places like women. While it is inconceivable to be a Ga man and to be uncircumcised, circumcision is a practice which differentiates Ga from neighbouring Akan peoples and which may partially explain the contempt with which Ga regard other ethnic groups.

At physiological puberty, ceremonies are performed for both males and females (*dzengnii*, world's things) which mark the transition from social immaturity to maturity. The emphasis in these ceremonies is on purification and preparation for the assumption of the adult roles of spouse and parent. These ceremonies are seen by Ga as prerequisites to the ordered sexual relations of marriage. Without the performance of such ceremonial, a person would be 'immoral and stupid', and after death his soul would be unable to assume ancestral status.

Marriage constitutes a major transition in the process of social maturation for men and women. A first marriage is contracted by two sets of ceremonies: betrothal (*shibimọ*) and wedding (*kpeemọ*) rites. Betrothal, which involves the transfer of goods from the groom's kin to the bride's family, established the groom's exclusive rights to the bride's sexuality and his kindred's rights to her reproductive capacity. The wedding, which entails a week of feasting, begins with the formal transfer of the bride to the groom's family and ends with a blessing at the shrine of the senior *kpele* god in Accra, *Nai we*. Wedding ceremonies are performed only for the first marriage of both partners. While these ceremonies confer prestige on the participants, they are not essential for establishing the legality of the alliance or the legitimacy of children, both of which are achieved by the betrothal ceremony.

Finally, funerary rites mark the gradual disassociation of the spirit from the body and the transition of the spirit from the status of living kinsmen to that of revered ancestral shade. The funerary rites begin with the ritual surrounding burial and conclude a year or more later with a feast. At the completion of these ceremonies, the soul has terminated its earthly existence, though not its earthly relations.

In order to comprehend this ultimate bio-social transition, certain Ga conceptions of person are relevant. According to the Ga, a person has two aspects: a body and a soul. While the body has only temporary existence, the soul (*susuma*) has eternal life. Although the soul's association with the body is limited, it is believed that every soul has a predetermined length of human existence. When a person dies prematurely or violently, an initial concern of the living is whether or not the soul has lived its allotted span.

During a person's lifetime the soul is associated with the body except in sleep, when it may leave the body and journey without limitations of time or space. The well-being of a person depends on the health of the physical body and of the soul. When a person is ill, Ga believe that his 'soul is bent down'. A traditional healer (*tsofatsẹ*) endeavours to cure the physical complaint and to raise the soul, for if the soul is not raised, the person will die.

After a person's death, the soul continues to be associated with the body for three days. When the soul leaves the body, it wanders 'nobody knows where' until the final funeral rites (*faafo*) are performed a year or more later. At these final rites the soul 'crosses the river' to join the ancestral shades. The world of the shades (*gbohiiadzeng*, dead persons' world) is not sharply defined by the Ga. It is believed that a person has the same social status in death as in life: a chief is chief, a commoner is commoner. The shades may manifest themselves to the living either in human form or in dreams; their spiritual presence may be invoked on certain occasions to assist the living. While the soul is the immortal aspect of a person, the physiological body involves the soul in certain inextricable relations. The blood which a person derives from his parents ties him to people and groups in Ga society during his lifetime, and after death his soul continues to be concerned with the affairs of these same social units.

The central concern of the cycle of life crisis ceremonies is the continuity of ordered relations between human beings. I discuss the sociological implications of these ceremonies from two analytical viewpoints. I first consider the cycle of ceremonies as a unit which differentiates basic social categories and groups in Ga society; I then analyse ceremonies as events specific to particular individuals in order to elucidate some of the implications of the ordering of ritual groups. These two analytical approaches are complementary, for each illuminates different aspects of the social significance of the cycle of life crisis ceremonies.

Viewed as a unit, the cycle of life crisis ceremonies distinguishes various social categories and groups in Ga society. These include ethnic affiliation and intratribal differences, living and dead people, men and women, and patrilateral kin and matrilateral kin. While Ga would accept these distinctions, they do not make them systematically. Nevertheless, these distinctions are implicit in certain ritual acts and explicit in others.

The cycle of ceremonies expresses the ethnic identity of the Ga people. Ga consider that their life crisis ceremonies distinguish them from other Ghanaian peoples and that similar ritual should be performed for each Ga person during his lifetime. Probably comparative analysis would show that the differences between Ga and non-Ga ritual for similar social transitions are less than the Ga assume. Certainly, there is considerable variation in the performance of the same life crisis ceremonies among the Ga. These variations arise in part from the lack of prescribed ritual and in part from differences in the ritual knowledge of celebrants. For each of the ceremonies, a general sequence of ritual acts should be observed, but within these limits considerable latitude exists. For example, at the betrothal ceremony, female cognates of the groom present a sum of money and other goods to the bride's kinswomen. Neither the manner of presenting these gifts nor the words with which they are proffered and received are prescribed. The presentation of the gifts may be preceded either by a lengthy introduction and prayer or by a few prefatory remarks. The most formally structured life crisis ceremony is probably the naming rite, but the celebrants of different ceremonies may vary in their familiarity with the customary ritual acts. Nevertheless, the Ga believe that the life crisis ceremonies which they perform are distinctive to Ga culture and that similar social transitions for different individuals are marked by similar

Preparing for a betrothal ceremony.

ritual. On the basis of these beliefs, the cycle of ceremonies may be said to express Ga identity.

Although the cycle of ceremonies as a unit is believed to distinguish Ga culture from other Ghanaian cultures, puberty rites are considered to reflect the heterogeneous ethnic origins of the contemporary Ga people. Each of the six types of female puberty rites is associated with a different cultural origin: Ga, Awutu, Guang, Adangme, Fanti, and Akwamu. The type of rite which is performed for a girl depends upon the purported origin of her father's paternal family (*we*). The general structure of these ceremonies is similar: purificatory ritual and feasting precede a period of confinement during which the girl is instructed in the proper conduct of a wife and mother. The ceremonies differ in ritual detail; the 'true Ga' maiden (*tungyoo*, camwood woman) is besmeared with red clay while the Adangme girl (*otofuyoo*, ceremonial hat woman) wears a special hat after the shaving of her head during the purificatory rite. Thus, female puberty rites express traditional cultural differences within Ga society.[4]

Another basic distinction which life crisis ceremonies convey is between living people and dead people. Since both categories of human being are believed to participate in these ceremonies, the continuity of relations between these two categories is a main theme of the ceremonies. In Ga thought, the ancestral shades are the moral guardians of the conduct of the living. The spirit (*susuma*) of a person who has not undergone puberty ritual and final funerary rites (*faafo*) cannot assume ancestral status. Puberty rites are perceived as prerequisites to

Presentation of the groom's gifts.

spiritual and social morality in adulthood, for they both 'wash away natural pollution (*adeboo mudzi*)' and inculcate moral norms for adult men and women. Without such ritual the final funerary rites (*faafo*) which mark the achievement of the highest and ultimate social status, the status of ancestral shade, cannot be performed. As the moral guardians of Ga society, the shades are called by the living to witness and sanction the performance of life crisis ritual. The naming ceremony, for example, opens with the symbolic summoning of the ancestral shade: pouring water before each door inside the compound, the senior patrikinsman of the baby requests the shades to attend.[5] At other life crisis ceremonies, the presence of the shades is enjoined by prayer and libation. Life crisis rituals, therefore, express the interdependence of living and dead and the authority of the dead over the living.

Sexual differentiation constitutes another important categorical differentiation in life crisis ceremonies. Apart from circumcision, which establishes masculine identity, the status transitions are similar for both sexes. The sex of the initiand, however, determines ritual variations. Certain variations express the solidarity of persons of the same sex. At the naming ceremony, for example, a person of the same sex as the infant introduces it to the essential elements of the Ga universe: namely, light, which is associated with the supreme being and immortality, earth, which is associated with biological existence and mortality, and water, which is associated with the means of continuing life. The selection of the person who makes this symbolic introduction is important, for Ga believe that through his touch he transmits his character to the infant.

Other ritual variations express male superordination and female subordination in Ga society. This aspect of the relations between the sexes is particularly clear in funerary ritual. When a man dies, his senior wife clasps his feet while his body is prepared for burial and all his wives are confined with his kinswomen during the twelve-week mourning period. When a woman dies, her husband observes neither ritual duties nor restrictions. Moreover, days of the week are divided into male days (*nuugbi*) and female days (*yoogbi*). Naming, circumcision, and puberty ceremonies must be performed on the same day of the week as the initiand's birth; such rites, therefore, may be observed on either male or female days. Marital and funerary rites, however, are restricted to female days, which are Monday, Thursday, and Saturday. Ga people explain this prescription by saying that male days are for the gods; in fact, however, ritual for certain gods is performed on female days.[6] Nevertheless, the explanation of this restriction is consistent with the subordinate status of life crisis ritual which involves relations between the living and the dead and the superior status of communal religious ritual which concerns relations between divine beings and men.

The final categorical distinction which I wish to consider is the differentiation of cognates into patrilateral and matrilateral kin. As I have mentioned, in Ga thought patrilateral kin are superordinate to matrilateral kin. The asymmetrical relationship between the two categories of cognates is variously expressed at all life cycle ceremonies. The nature of the relationship between matrilateral and patrilateral cognates is symbolized explicitly in the naming ceremony. After the infant has been introduced to the essential elements of the Ga universe and blessed, its kinship affiliation is defined and acknowledged. All the celebrants raise their hands to their right shoulders, then to their left shoulders, and finally to their breasts. This ritual act symbolizes the child's successive entrance into its patrilateral families, matrilateral families, and total kindred. The association of right with patrilateral kinship and left with matrilateral kinship is expressed in the seating arrangements at all life crisis ceremonies. Moreover, the association of right with superordinate status and left with subordinate status also pertains to the dichotomy of sex, for women, as I have noted, are referred to as 'left-handed people (*abekulǫi*)'. The superordination of patrilateral kin to matrilateral kin is expressed implicitly in the ritual precedence of patrikinsmen at all life cycle ceremonies: the rituals are performed in houses belonging to patrikinsmen; patrikinsmen perform ritual acts before matrikinsmen; at each ceremony a larger number of patrikinsmen than matrikinsmen have ritual duties. Ultimately, the superordination of patrikinsmen to matrikinsmen is related to Ga ideas concerning the physiology of kinship, which include the notion that a greater proportion of a person's blood comes from his father than from his mother.

Thus far, my analysis of life crisis ritual has concerned the expression of social categories and their relations in ritual acts. I have focused on social ideas which are symbolized within the context of the ceremonial cycle. Certain of these ideas, such as intra-ethnic variation, are restricted to one ceremony; others, such as differentiation of matrilateral kin and patrilateral kin, are repeated in every ceremony. My consideration of social ideas, however, represents only one aspect of the analysis of life crisis ceremonies; another aspect concerns the ordering of ritual groups and their wider social effects.

The performance of each life crisis ceremony is specific to an individual at a particular transition in his social maturation. As a person matures, the composition of the ritual group changes to incorporate new sets of relations. Throughout a person's life, cognatic affiliation with him is the major principle for organizing ritual groups at his life crisis ceremonies. After the initiand's marriage, however, the participation of affines is also required. Authority within ritual groups, however, rests with genealogically senior cognates in general and patrilateral kinsmen in particular. Ritual groups are necessarily ephemeral; they come into being for a specific occasion and dissolve at the close of the ceremony.

The transitory nature of ritual groups has certain important implications for the ordering of relations between social units. On the one hand, life crisis ceremonies express cleavages between kin units, particularly *shiai*; on the other hand, they serve to integrate the Ga community through a ramifying network of cognatic and affinal ties. The performance of a ceremony expresses the kin units to which the initiand belongs and relations between these groups. The kin unit which is patrilateral in one ritual context, however, may be matrilateral in another. Further, the kin units associated in one ritual context are unlikely to be in another. Since the kindreds of only full siblings are similar, in different ritual contexts an individual participates with different cognates and non-cognates. Ultimately, the performance of life crisis ceremonial implies a network of cognatic relations linking individual and groups throughout the Ga community of Central Accra.

New Ideas and the Ceremonial Cycle

I now turn to a consideration of the adaptation of the traditional cycle of life crisis ceremonies to ideas associated with the modernization process. Three sets of ideas are particularly relevant: Christianity, friendship, and affluence. Each of the three concepts has a variety of meanings. Any one of which may be primary for an individual; different ones may be used by the same person in different social contexts. Before discussing the relations between these ideas and traditional ritual, I consider briefly the variant meanings of these concepts, some of the ways in which individuals use them, and their significance for ordering social relations.

The identification of a person as a Christian has at least four alternative meanings. It may be used either as a categorical label or as a standard for behaviour; it may be used to refer either to participation in Christian ritual of to adherence to a system of thought. As a categorical label, it is used to differentiate certain people from others who are 'pagan'. The minimal implication of this use of the term is that the person at one time either attended a mission school or was baptized in a Christian sect. When the term is used in this way, it frequently has an evaluative connotation which is that Christians are superior to pagans. As a standard of behaviour, Christianity is also used in an evaluative sense. People may explain their own ideas and behaviour or those of others in terms of being a Christian. Thus, a person may say that he knows nothing about a traditional ceremony, such as puberty ritual, that he does not observe a traditional ceremony such as the Rite of Feasting (*Homowo*), or that he does not believe in witches, because he is a Christian. To postulate Christianity as a standard of behaviour is a way of rationalizing the behaviour of oneself or of others, but it is a flexible standard. While one person might find it a satisfactory explanation for certain behaviour, another might not. For Christian Ga, these two meanings of being Christian as a category term and as a standard of behaviour have a positive connotation which ultimately derives from the association of Christianity with Western culture.

A third meaning of being a Christian is participation in the activites of a Christian sect. Such activities may include attendance at services of worship, membership in church study groups, and participation in evangelical work. In contemporary Accra, there are three main categories of Christian sect: established sects such as the Church of

England and the Methodist Church, fundamentalist sects such as Jehovah's Witnesses, and 'spiritual' churches. The established sects dating from the nineteenth century in Accra have the greatest numerical strength. In order to survive and grow, these churches have developed considerable tolerance of traditional custom; the general attitude of such churches has been to discourage traditional ritual but to prohibit only practices which directly interfere with Christian ritual. Thus, the fact of polygynous unions has been recognized if not positively sanctioned. Only a monogamous man may be a full communicant in Anglican and Methodist ritual; a devout woman married to a polygynous man may have her marriage 'blessed' in church which entitles her to use the honorific title 'Mrs.'. One social effect of the latitude which established sects give to traditional customs is that their membership encompasses the range of socio-economic categories among the Ga of Central Accra. By contrast, the fundamentalist sects which have gained adherents in the period since the Second World War have been much less permissive to traditional institutions; consequently, their membership is restricted to white-collar occupational categories. The 'spiritual' churches, which have developed throughout West Africa, paricularly since 1945, in response to intensified modernization pressures, consciously fuse traditional and Christian ritual and accept the contemporary social system. While their membership includes a wide range of socio-economic categories, it is drawn principally from those who aspire to higher status in the new socio-economic order, such as young clerks, school leavers, and market women. These cults depend for their success on the charisma of their 'prophets'; their membership fluctuates and individuals circulate from cult to cult; internal power struggles occur frequently and often lead to the fragmentation of sects.

The multiplicity of sects in Accra has a number of implications for participation in Christian ritual. One consequence is transitory membership in different sects. Although it is possible for a person to be a life-long adherent of one sect, it is common for people to belong sequentially to a number of different churches. The usual pattern at present is to join an established sect as a child and to transfer one's allegiance to a fundamentalist sect or spiritual church later in life. Each type of church satisfies different needs and individuals search for the one which is most congenial to them. In general, the appeal of the established sects is due to their formal ritual and status as the oldest sects in Accra; the fundamentalist sects offer rigid puritanical standards of conduct which are equated with sophistication and Western ideas, and the spiritual churches are noted for their personalism, that is, interest in the problems of individual communicants. Transferring denominational allegiance constitutes one type of change in participation in Christian ritual; another is transferring membership from one congregation to another within a sect, which may be associated with status aspirations. For example, Ga attend one of two Anglican churches in Central Accra; at St. Mary's Church the service is conducted in Ga and the worshippers are all Ga speakers; at the Anglican Cathedral the services are in English, the worshippers include Europeans, members of the African élite, and others who understand English and prefer the 'high church' ritual. Changing congregations for prestige reasons probably pertains to people who belong to established sects, whereas changing congregational membership may also be related to the fragmentation of sects within 'spiritual' churches. In the latter case, certain members of the original congregation may follow a prophet who breaks away from the founder: such a congregational transfer does not imply status considerations but rather attachment to a particular individual.

The fourth meaning of Christianity refers to adherence to a particular system of thought. Probably this meaning of being a Christian is limited to a fairly small group of devout Christians who concern themselves with the ideas expressed in Christian doctrine. In certain respects Christian beliefs are not antithetical to Ga religious beliefs. Beliefs in a supreme deity, the immortality of the human soul, divine justice, social reciprocity within the community of believers are shared by both systems of thought. Such complementary concepts have facilitated the acceptance of Christianity by Ga. At the same time, however, other Christian ideas, such as the value of monogamy, the deprecation of traditional ritual practices, and the castigation of other Christian sects, have hindered the acceptance of Christianity.

The several meanings of Christianity or being a Christian are not mutually exclusive. Any one of them may be appropriate to the same inidividual in different contexts. Only one of them may be applicable to a particular person in any situation. Nevertheless, the order in which these meanings have been discussed probably corresponds to their rank-ordering in Ga society. The use of 'Christian' as a categorical label pertains to a majority of the Ghana Ga population, Christianity as a standard of behaviour to a lesser number of Ga, as participation in Christian ritual to an even smaller number, and as adherence to a system of thought to the smallest number of Christian Ga. All of these meanings, however, refer to a Western institution which, as I shall discuss below, has significant implications for the performance of traditional ritual.

New concepts of association deriving from the modernization process constitute a second set of new social ideas. The most important of these for contemporary Ga ritual is friendship. Friendship may be defined as a dyadic relationship between persons of the same sex, equivalent age, and similar socio-economic status. The relationship is established in the context of groups which are not based on traditional principles of kinship and authority, such as occupational groups, Christian churches, and athletic groups. While friendships are established in the context of such organized groups, they are expressed and developed in leisure situations, such as visiting, drinking in bars, and ritual events. Within the Ga community the concept of friendship tends to be restricted to members of the younger age categories. While younger people frequently mention 'tight friends', elderly people often say that they do not have any friends. Further discussion and observation, however, usually discloses that the latter have many of the relationships which the former classify as friendship. The salient point, however, is that often these relationships have bases in attenuated blood kinship ties which are of primary significance to the older Ga person and which he perceives as the basis for the relationship, but which the younger Ga person disregards, as the following cases illustrate.

One elderly man who is a retired civil servant, a member of the Ga royal council and an active participant in an established church says that he does not have any friends. Yet daily people come to visit him to inquire about his health, to inform him of developments in traditional politics, to request his financial assistance, to discuss personal and political problems. In conversation, he often mentions people with whom he has worked and members of literary and political discussion groups to which he has belonged. When he walks through the streets, he continually stops to greet acquaintances. Significantly, however, when he encounters a child, he asks the names of its parents and their families, thereby placing the child within the traditional kinship structure. His point of reference is not the emerging Westernized society, but the traditional Ga society and, therefore, he does not define any of his relationships as friendship. One 'young' man in his mid-thirties who works as a clerk in a government department, is the organizer of a football team, and has always lived in Central Accra except for two years, when his department sent him to Ashanti, refers often to his 'friends'. This man, who was a schoolboy during the Second World War, takes pride in his interest in 'strangers' which dates from his experience with Afro-American soldiers; he refers to such men and members of the African diplomatic corps as friends. One of his intimates is a patrilateral kinsman who works in another government department and now lives in a suburb of Accra, but is an organizer of the same football team and spends most of his leisure time in the same cobbler's shop, which serves as a *rendez-vous* for young men in the neighbourhood. These two men refer to each other as 'friends', though occasionally when discussing Ga culture, they refer to one another as 'cousins'. Such a person's aspirations are associated with western technological society and one of the ways he expresses these interests is by using friendship as a basic category for social relationships, even for those which originate in kinship bonds.

A third set of ideas concerns prestige based on achieved status rather than ascribed status. In their extreme form such ideas are expressed in the 'big man' complex. The big man is a person who establishes prestige and influence among his peers and subordinates by spending money. His affluence is reflected in his patterns of consumption and expenditure. He buys Western goods, such as imported liquors, foodstuffs, cloth, automobiles, and household furnishings. His style of life is expensive and expansive; he lives in a large concrete house and may own several others which he rents; he has access to desirable women, gives big 'drinks' parties, and attends expensive nightclubs. Access to this way of life depends upon money, either fluid or credit, and derives usually from high status in the modern political system and/or Western education and status in the modern economic sector of society. The big man's largesse is both a means of expressing his social status and one of establishing relations of dependence with less affluent persons. His dependents regard him with ambivalence. They admire his style of life and aspire to emulate it, but they are cynical about the means by which he acquires his wealth.

Although there are few big men, the big man is the model for many. Consequently, people strive to stress their affluence in similar ways, even if they become inextricably involved in debt and credit relationships. Throughout the society, positive value is attached to imported goods. Imported liquors are preferred to similar locally distilled products; junior civil servants living in small rooms in family houses in Central Accra furnish their rooms with large wireless sets, refrigerators, and various other products of Western technology, which are purchased on credit. The value placed on the consumption and distribution of Western goods is related to the association of such commodities with modern society.

In general, the cycle of life crisis ceremonies has been extremely receptive to those ideas which have developed within the context of the modernization process. This receptivity is related to a number of factors which include the basic concern of these ceremonies with the relations between the living and the dead, the informal structure of traditional ceremonial, and the nature of the ritual groups which are based on the initiand's kindred. Two modes of adaptation are characteristic of life crisis ritual: the modification of the cycle of ceremonies and the expression of new ideas in ritual. The comparative ease with which these adjustments have been made accounts for the universal practice of these ceremonies within the contemporary Ga community.

Although these two types of ritual adaptation are distinct processes, they are manifestations of the same modernizing ideas. The three sets of ideas expressed in contemporary secular ritual are: the religious affiliation of the initiand, friendship as a basis for association, and prestige within the emerging socio-economic order. Certain aspects of one or more sets are expressed in every contemporary ceremony. In the following analysis, I discuss the relation of these new ideas to the modification of the ceremonial cycle and how these new ideas find ritual expression.

The ceremonial cycle has been modified in two ways: certain rites are rarely observed today and new rites have been introduced. The two ceremonies which are celebrated very occasionally are the traditional wedding ceremony (*kpeemɔ*) and puberty ceremonies (*dzengnii*). Among the three new ceremonies, the church wedding is in part a substitution for the traditional wedding, while the afternoon naming ceremony (*shwane kpodziemɔ*) and the funerary memorial ceremony are supplementary rites, for these innovations do not replace any ceremony but are performed in addition to traditional naming and funerary rites. From case histories and conversations with Ga, it appears that these changes have occurred during the past fifty years which is also the period of intensified relations between Ga society and Western technological society.

Given the traditional belief that puberty rites are prerequisite to ancestral status and the continuing significance of beliefs in ancestral shades, the infrequent performance of puberty rites in contemporary Central Accra is anomalous. Not only are puberty rites rarely observed, but many Ga are unaware that such ceremonies may be performed for boys as well as girls. The usual explanation for not performing puberty ritual is that it is something which Christians do not do. Since the same rationalization might be offered for any other traditional ceremony, the cogency of this explanation is disputable. A more satisfactory explanation is found in the meaning of the ceremony in traditional society. By comparison with many other African societies, puberty ritual has a limited purpose in Ga society. Such ceremonies mark the transition from social immaturity to social maturity, but they do not establish sexual identity: this is achieved by male circumcision earlier in life.[7] Probably today the status transition from social immaturity to maturity is expressed in different ways. For many young people, leaving middle school and assuming a wage-earning occupation symbolize the same transition, albeit at a slightly older age. Since more boys than girls attend school, one would expect to find puberty ceremonies performed more often for girls than boys, as is in fact the case. Probably the performance of male puberty ceremonies is restricted to the holders of certain traditional offices, for whom such ritual is observed as part of their initiation to office. The priests of the two senior gods in Accra had these rites performed when they assumed office in their mid-forties. Female puberty rites are likely to be observed either for uneducated girls or for girls whose parents are particularly interested in Ga traditional culture.

Like puberty rites, traditional wedding rites are observed infrequently, if at all. Various factors account for the non-performance of this ceremony. First, it does not establish a marriage; this is contracted at the betrothal ceremony (*shibimǫ*) which is universally observed in contemporary Ga society. A second consideration is the diminishing significance of traditional religion for most people in Central Accra, for the culmination of the traditional wedding was the blessing of the couple by the priest of the senior god in Accra. A third factor of importance is the prestige associated with the traditional wedding ceremony. The performance of the traditional wedding ceremony conferred prestige on both bride and groom, but particularly on the bride. Its observance was restricted to the first marriage of both spouses, though other considerations, such as the status of the bride's family and the wealth of the groom's, were probably relevant. The contemporary church wedding may be considered as a substitute for the traditional wedding ceremony for reasons of prestige. Church weddings are restricted to high socio-economic status categories, such as senior civil servants and professional persons. Apart from the prestige which such a rite confers on the bride, there are formal parallels with traditional ritual. Feasting and the offering of advice to the couple are integral parts of traditional and modern wedding ceremonies.

The two supplementary life crisis ceremonies which are widely practised in contemporary Accra are the afternoon naming ceremony and the 'memorial service' for deceased Christians. Although the traditional pre-dawn naming rite is always observed, young men often perform an additional afternoon naming ceremony, especially if the baby is their first child. An afternoon naming ceremony is a party to which the youth invites many friends as well as relatives. He hires a dance band and liquor flows freely. Although such a party may be given on the same day as the traditional naming rite, it is often postponed until the beginning of the month, when salaries are paid. If an afternoon naming rite is to be held, donations are deferred until that occasion. An afternoon naming ceremony is considered to be a financial gamble, for it involves considerable expense for the new father, and if he is unlucky, he may receive little assistance in recouping his losses, for 'some people just come to drink and don't give anything'. Traditionally oriented Ga look with disdain upon this ceremonial innovation, but it has become a fairly widespread practice, particularly among members of white-collar and professional status categories. The ceremony is one way of establishing prestige for oneself among one's contemporaries and of having a good time in the modern idiom.

While the performance of an afternoon naming ceremony is restricted to young fathers, a universal innovation for deceased Christians is the 'memorial service'. This ceremony is observed during the official twelve-week mourning period following death. Most memorial services occur on the first and last Sundays of the month; at the conclusion of the regular church service, the minister announces the names and gives brief biographical sketches of the people whose memorial services are being celebrated that day. After the service the relatives and affines of the deceased greet the members of the congregation outside the church. The family and friends, who may number two hundred or more, then go to the family house of the deceased, where refreshments are served and donations may be presented. The mourners may stay until late in the afternoon.

These alterations in the cycle of ceremonies reflect aspects of the impact of the modernization process on life crisis ritual. Within the context of every contemperary ceremony, however, one or more sets of new ideas may be expressed in various ways. These ideas may be stated explicitly in ritual acts and implicitly in the use of certain material goods and in the social structure of the ritual group. Such manifestations of modern ideas not only reflect the adaptation of life crisis ritual to new ideas but express the achieved status or status aspirations of either the initiand or the celebrants who perform the rite on his behalf. Moreover, they indicate the development of non-kin bases of social alignment which in the context of life crisis ritual supplement kin relations but in the wider social system may eventually compete with kin relations as major organizing principles within the Ga community of Central Accra.

Ideas associated with Christianity are expressed in ritual acts and in the use of certain objects in life crisis ceremonies. The central idea of importance is the religious affiliation of the initiand and of kinsmen who perform the ceremony. If the initiand is a Christian, not only will certain rites be observed, such as a memorial service or possibly a church wedding and funeral, but ritual variations may be introduced into traditional ceremonies. In certain devout Christian families, for example, Christian prayers, hymns, and biblical readings may form part of the betrothal ceremony. In the betrothal ceremony, the Christian status of the bride is symbolized by the presentation of a ring, prayer book, and hymnal in addition to the customary prestations of money and beverages. Similarly, the burial of a Christian differs from that of a 'pagan' in the use of a hearse rather than of pall bearers to transport the corpse from the family house to the cemetery. These are the principal means by which the Christian affiliation of the initiand may be expressed in life crisis ritual.

The Christian status of the initiand implies that certain ritual innovations may be made in life crisis ceremonies. Whether or not these innovations are observed in a particular ritual performance depends on a consideration of other factors. These include conflicts of status, as well as socio-economic considerations. The status of an initiand as a Christian may be perceived as less important than another status which he also occupies and which would be considered of primary significance in a cermony. When one of the Accra sub-chiefs died, his coffin was carried to the cemetery by pall bearers rather than in a hearse; in this case his status as a traditional office-holder took precedence over his status as a Christian. Although the difference between a hearse and pall bearers may appear minor, various significant ideas and practices are associated with this distinction. When pall bearers carry a coffin, the spirit of the deceased is said to force them to pass throughout the town to bid farewell to its kinsmen and acquaintances in their own houses before proceeding to the cemetery; by contrast, a hearse drives straight from the house to the cemetery. The use of pall bearers is one way of expressing and affirming networks of association within the community; whereas the use of a hearse focuses on the deceased as an individual rather than as a part of a system of relationships.

Variations in ritual are also related to socio-economic factors. A church wedding entails expenses which many people can not afford. Such rites, therefore, are restricted to members of senior civil servant and professional occupational categories. Not only do these ceremonies symbolize affluence, but they also imply membership or aspiration for membership in a national élite which patterns its domestic relations on a Western model rather than on a traditional Ga model. Thus, while the Christian status of the initiand opens a range of possibilities for the modification of life crisis ritual, the modifications in the observance of a particular rite frequently depend on other considerations.

Another set of modernizing ideas expressed in life crisis ritual is found in new forms of interpersonal relations based on non-kinship principles. Within the context of life crisis ritual, the relevant relationship is friendship. Friends may be invited to attend a life crisis ceremony either as observers or as officiants. The former role is more usual than the latter. Nevertheless, at the naming ceremony of an infant, a close friend of one of the child's parents may be requested to show the child to the morning star; traditionally, an esteemed senior kinsman of the same sex as the infant assumes this role. Since the role concerns the introduction of the child to the Ga universe rather than to its kindred, it is one which a non-kinsman may fulfill. Similarly, at the betrothal ceremony, an articulate friend of the mother of either the bride or the groom may be invited to speak for the women of that 'side'. Associations based upon bonds of friendship are particularly apparent at the various funerary rites. The network of association is much wider than at any other life cycle ceremony. Not only are close kinsmen involved but friends and associates attend.

At least one of the major voluntary associations of Ga women in Accra arose in response to the requirements of funerary ceremonies. *Nanęimęi Akpee* (Friends Society) was the largest voluntary association in Accra in 1954. At that time it had as official membership of 3,000; in 1965, it was about one tenth that size. The inspiration for this society came when five traders were returning from a memorial service and saw an old woman carrying her own stool; they decided to form an organization which would help bereaved members by providing seats, refreshments, and choral music on such occasions. In its heyday, *Nanęimęi Akpee* had branches in Ga communities in all the major towns in Ghana. The society began to decline when another organization with similar purposes was formed, *Nyęmimęi Akpee* (Siblings' Society). By 1965, however, *Nanęimęi Akpee* was beginning to flourish again and continued to assist bereaved members.

In Central Accra, Ga attend funerary rites in part because they wish to show their respect for the deceased and his kin and to enjoy seeing their acquaintances, and in part because they feel obligated by explicit rules of reciprocity. These rules are expressed in the presentation of donations. Whenever donations are made, a careful record is kept of the donors and the amount of money given by each. Should a donor be bereaved, former recipients must at least match the original contribution. Yet donations are rarely sufficient to meet the cost of a funeral and the financial burden falls on close cognates, especially mature children of the deceased.

While the inclusion of friends in life crisis ritual groups changes the structure of the group from one based solely on consanguineal and affinal affiliations with the initiand, friendship relations are subordinate to kin relations. Responsibility for the observation of a rite rests with senior kinsmen and only one or two ritual roles are allocated to friends at any ceremony. Further, the number of kin exceeds the number of friends present at a life crisis ceremony. Nevertheless, the inclusion of friends in ritual groups implies networks of interpersonal association which are alternatives to kin networks. Moreover, since friendship has been defined as a relationship between approximate socio-economic equals, the friendship networks express emerging class distinctions within the Ga community.

While friendship networks reflect incipient class cleavages within the

Collecting donations at a funeral.

Ga community of Central Accra, the limitations which kin relations place on this development is also expressed in life crisis ceremonies. These ceremonies constitute a visual statement of asymmetrical class structure among kinsmen. The kinsmen who attend are present by virtue of their blood kinship with the initiand. In their dress and deportment, however, a wide range of socio-economic levels are symbolized. At betrothal ceremonies extremely wealthy women dressed in modish satin gowns and diamond jewels sit beside poor women with faded and ill-matched dresses and bare feet. Hair-dos range from sophisticated straightened hair styles and wigs to traditionally plaited hair styles and head-ties. On these ceremonial occasions, however, deference is paid to ascribed status based on age and consanguineal proximity to the contracting parties rather than to achieved status within the modern economic sphere. Thus, life cycle ritual groups express both emerging class categories and the restrictions which kin relations as the superordinate basis for association place on the full development of a class structure based on social groups.

The consideration of class status is related to the third set of ideas, concepts concerning prestige based on achieved status rather than ascribed status. Such ideas are expressed not only in the performance of certain ceremonies such as the afternoon naming ceremony and the church marriage service, but in the expenditures which ceremonies entail. Financial expenditure as manifested either explicitly in cash at betrothal ceremonies or implicitly in the amount and quality of material goods used in any ceremony reflect either the actual status of the donor or his status aspirations. Such considerations are clearly expressed at betrothal ceremonies. According to tradition, the entire betrothal expenses for the groom should be less than £30. The expenses of five betrothals on which data are available range from £37 to £226. The financial variations accord with variations in the socio-economic status of the contracting parties: £37 for the betrothal of a junior civil servant and an illiterate trader; £56 and £94 for those of two sets of junior civil servants; £190 for that of a senior civil servant and a teacher, and £226 for that of two medical doctors.

While the amassing of the necessary funds for such expenditures is the responsibility of one individual, the kin group to which he belongs also derives enhanced status and prestige from his affluence. This is expressed in the joking at betrothal ceremonies. The two groups of women exchange light-hearted banter during the counting of each donation and the serving of refreshments. One of the themes of such remarks is the groom's family's affluence and sophistication which is phrased in terms of European standards, as the following comments recorded at two betrothal rites illustrate.

'All these are good drinks. They are European drinks'.
'We are doing this, because we come from a better family'.
'We come from overseas. Yesterday they brought the ring in an airplane — a VC 10'.

Such competitive joking has significant implications for the limitations which kin affiliations place on individual social mobility. The joking expresses the identification of the members of kin groups with the individual. The group as a whole shares in the prestige accruing to the individual from his ability to symbolize his achieved or aspired status through the use of money. The attainment of higher socio-economic status by the individual, however, is restricted by the extent to which kinsmen consider that he is under an obligation to assist less affluent relatives and the pressures which they can exert to enforce his compliance with their expectations. The ability of an individual to sever himself from such obligations is limited within such a long-established community as that of the Ga in Central Accra, in which kinship ideas and principles constitute the fundamental bases of interpersonal relations.

My discussion of the adaptation of the cycle of life crisis ceremonies to modern ideas has implications for the persistence of these ceremonies within the Ga community of Central Accra. The apparent ease with which the ritual system has assimilated new concepts suggests that the cycle will continue to be performed and to adapt to new sources of social change. The cycle may be increasingly modified. Certain ceremonies may cease to be observed and new ceremonies may be introduced. At any given time, however, the relevant life cycle transitions will be ceremonialized in ritual which is rationalized as part of the traditional life crisis cycle of ceremonies. At present the underlying premise of the ceremonial cycle is that the ceremonies must be performed if one is a Ga. They therefore establish and affirm the ethnic identity of individuals. Although it is possible that with the development of a national identity, ethnic identity would cease to be a relevant concept; the probability of such a development is extremely remote. For the foreseeable future, therefore, life crisis ceremonies associated with ethnic identification will continue to be performed by the Ga and other Ghanaian peoples.

In summary, my concern in this chapter has been to discuss various aspects of the relations between ritual and social systems. The first part considers not only how ceremonies express the relations between social categories and units in ritual acts, but how the organization of ritual groups relates to the organization of individuals and social units in the wider social system. The second part discusses the effect of changes in social ideas on ritual systems both at the level of ideas expressed in ritual acts and at the level of the structure of ritual. This analysis, however, does not assume that ritual mirrors society in such a way that within the context of ritual all significant social ideas are expressed; nor does it assume that all ideas of ritual importance are socially significant. Rather it assumes that ritual may express certain basic social ideas. The extent to which ritual incorporates and expresses such ideas relates to the meaningfulness of ritual to individuals and the use which they make of it.

The Ga case clearly illustrates these processes. Ritual is perceived by Ga to be necessary for establishing and maintaining order between categories of being. Life crisis ceremonies involve orderly relations between the living and the dead. Since life crisis ritual groups are transitory groups composed of the initiands' cognates and affines, the performance of life crisis ritual integrates individuals into a ramifying network of community-wide kin relations. The facility with which new ideas are incorporated in life crisis ritual means that individuals can use these ceremonies to symbolize new needs and aspirations and that the structure of life crisis ritual groups expresses new bases of social alignment within the community. Nevertheless, the persistence of the cycle of life crisis ceremonies in contemporary Central Accra is related to the continuing relevance of traditional social ideas, principles, and relationships within the Ga community. These, in turn, are associated with certain underlying economic and demographic factors, which include the longevity and stability of the Ga population and the comparative lack of economic differentiation within the Ga community of Central Accra.

REFERENCES

1. Evans-Pritchard distinguishes between collective and personal rites in his discussion of Nuer sacrifice. 'These terms draw attention to the formal distinction between sacrifices offered for persons and those offered on behalf of social groups'. (E. E. Evans-Pritchard, *Nuer Religion*, Oxford, 1956, p. 198).

2. In contrast to religious groups with stable personnel which I have described in *Kpele Lala*.

3. I have discussed the symbolism of one ceremony in 'The Ga Naming Rite', *Anthropos* **63/4**, 1968/9, pp. 904–20.

4. I lack information on differences in male puberty ritual.

5. This practice is related to the traditional custom of burying the dead within their paternal houses.

6. See *Kpele Lala*.

7. This explanation would account for the continuing importance of male initiation among Xhosa in East London (B. A. Pauw, *The Second Generation*, Cape Town, 1963, pp. 88–94).

CHAPTER V

THE GA KINSMAN'S CONCEPTS

Hitherto my discussion of continuity and change in Ga kinship in Central Accra has concerned the analysis of institutions and social units. The generality of these analyses and their emphasis on social groups, however, suggest that undue weighting may have been given to traditional factors. It may be that although individuals are constrained by their domestic arrangements and residence in Central Accra to conform overtly to certain traditional standards, traditional concepts do not have much relevance to individuals. If given a choice, individuals perhaps would respond in a less traditional manner than their social situations permit. Moreover, it may be that an analytical focus on social institutions and groups blurs the actual variation in adherence to traditional standards at the individual level within the Ga population of Central Accra. In this chapter I report an attempt to circumvent my biases as an ethnographer primarily concerned with understanding social institutions.

My analytical concern is with variations in adherence to traditional Ga culture within the Ga population of Central Accra. The basic questions with which I deal are: What is the nature of variation in adherence to Ga concepts? Is there a consistency between cultural variation and sociological factors? If such a consistency exists, how is it to be explained? My discussion rests upon a distinction between two modes of relating to culture involving qualitatively different processes. One mode involves the internalization of cultural ideas in such a way that these ideas constitute a person's cognitive structure. Such internalized ideas may be expressed as beliefs, as rules for behaviour, or as standardized ways of behaving in appropriate social contexts. The other mode of relating to culture concerns the ability to explain cultural ideas. Interpretative understanding of cultural ideas may or may not involve the internalization of these concepts. An analysis of the implications of the distinction between these two modes of relating to culture constitutes my theoretical focus in this chapter.

My discussion of variation in adherence to traditional Ga cultural standards is based on an analysis of responses to a standardized interview of open-ended questions. The questionnaire elicits information about the two modes of relating to culture. For the purposes of this analysis, the questions which concern internalized ideas and behaviour are termed 'participation questions'; those which pertain to the interpretative understanding of cultural concepts are termed 'knowledge questions'. The nineteen participation questions concerning secular and ritual issues; they include questions about social distance, observance of life crisis and *kpele* ritual, witchcraft, Christianity, utilization of traditional and Western medicine. The four knowledge questions inquire about the meaning of certain widely observed ritual acts; three are phrases from life crisis ceremonies and the fourth concerns the meaning of a preliminary purification ritual (*akpade*) at the annual Rite of Feasting (*Hǫmǫwǫ*). The responses to each question have been coded for traditionality according to a weighted scale. Consequently, there are two scores for each respondent: one a summation of participation response scores, the other a summation of knowledge response scores.

The questionnaire was administered in the Ga language to a socially differentiated sample of Ga living in Central Accra.[1] Five social criteria differentiate the sample of respondents: neighbourhood, sex, age, class, and household type.[2] I discuss these variables and my preliminary hypotheses concerning the relations between social attributes and response scores before examining the analytical findings of the survey.

Although Central Accra includes the old coastal Ga settlements in Accra, its present limits incorporate residential areas established during the last thirty years (see Chapter I). Moreover, while the population of Central Accra is predominantly Ga, the proportion of Ga within different parts of Central Accra varies considerably. Generally these variables are co-ordinate: the older the residential area, the larger the proportion of Ga inhabitants; the newer the neighbourhood, the smaller the proportion of Ga. In order to test hypotheses concerning the relations between adherence to traditional standards and the ethnic composition and longevity of residential areas, thirty-two respondents were interviewed in each of three parts of Central Accra: Ussher Town, James Town, and Riponsville.[3] This ordering of neighbourhoods represents a continuum from high to low concentrations of Ga and from old to new residential areas. I assume that the greater the proportion of Ga and the older the neighbourhood, the greater will be the probability of cultural continuity. It is hypothesised, therefore, that the proportion of respondents with high traditionality scores for both types of questions will be greatest in Ussher Town, medial in James Town, and least in Riponsville.

Since women have less access to Western education and thereby to the requisite skills for effective participation in an industrialized economy, it is likely that women will be more culturally conservative than men and that this will be reflected in a correlation between female sex and high traditionality scores for participation and knowledge questions.

Similarly, age has been chosen to test hypotheses on the association between cultural continuity and age. Twelve male and twelve female respondents were interviewed in each age category: 15–29 years, 30–44 years, 45–59 years and over 59 years. Given the increasing availability of Western education to younger people of both sexes, the intensified use of mass media in the past twenty years, the national political developments of the post-war period, and the association of seniority in years with authority within kin units which as I have noted includes responsibility for the performance of traditional life crisis ceremonial, it is probable that older people will be more traditionally oriented than younger people, and that this will be reflected in a correlation between high traditionality scores and older age categories.

Class, the fourth variable, is used to test hypotheses concerning relations between socio-economic status and adherence to traditional standards. This variable has been dichotomized: I or lower socio-economic status and II or higher socio-economic status. This classification is based on a consideration of two factors, education and occupation. Lower socio-economic status implies primary school education or less and either a traditional occupation such as farmer or fisherman or an unskilled or semi-skilled modern occupation such as labourer or trader. Higher socio-economic status implies at least a middle school education and a skilled modern occupation such as clerk or teacher.[4] The implications of socio-economic status for participation in the modern sector of Ghanaian society are such that adherence to traditional standards is likely to be associated with lower social class. Fifty-six of the respondents were of lower and forty of higher class status.

The final variable, house type, is divided into four categories.[5] These categories range from least to most traditional as conjugal family unit, bisexual kin unit with dependent conjugal family unit, bisexual kin unit, and unisexual kin unit (with nine, twenty, forty, and twenty-seven respondents, respectively). Changes in domestic organization are likely to be associated with changes in adherence to traditional ideas and practices, and this will be reflected in a correlation between non-traditional house type and low traditionality scores (see Table V/1).

A final preliminary hypothesis is that there is a positive correlation between participation and knowledge scores. That is, if a person has a high traditional participation score, it is anticipated that he also has a high traditional knowledge score, and conversely, that a person with a low participation score also has a low knowledge score. This hypothesis is based on the assumption that there is a consistency between cognitive patterns and the ability to explicate ideas.

TABLE V/1
DISTRIBUTION OF CATEGORIES OF RESPONDENTS

Age	Class	House Type	Ussher Town		James Town		Riponsville	
			Male	Female	Male	Female	Male	Female
15–29	I	1	—	—	—	—	—	—
		2	—	2	—	1	—	—
		3	—	1	2	—	—	—
		4	2	1	—	1	—	—
	II	1	—	—	—	1	1	1
		2	—	—	1	1	—	1
		3	2	—	1	—	3	2
		4	—	—	—	—	—	—
30–44	I	1	—	—	1	—	—	—
		2	—	—	—	2	—	—
		3	1	1	1	1	—	1
		4	1	3	—	—	—	2
	II	1	—	—	1	1	—	—
		2	—	—	—	—	1	1
		3	1	—	1	—	1	—
		4	1	—	—	2	—	—
45–59	I	1	—	—	—	—	—	—
		2	—	—	1	—	1	2
		3	—	3	—	1	—	1
		4	2	1	—	2	—	—
	II	1	—	—	1	—	—	—
		2	—	—	—	—	2	—
		3	—	—	2	—	1	1
		4	2	—	—	1	—	—
60+	I	1	—	—	—	—	—	—
		2	—	—	1	1	1	—
		3	1	2	2	2	1	1
		4	3	2	—	—	—	1
	II	1	—	—	—	—	1	1
		2	—	—	1	—	—	—
		3	—	—	—	1	1	1
		4	—	—	—	—	—	—

Key: Class I: primary school or less education and unskilled or traditional occupation; Class II: middle school or more education and white collar occupation. House type 1: conjugal family; 2: kin group with dependent conjugal family; 3: bisexual kin group; 4: unisexual kin group.

When these preliminary hypotheses are tested statistically, the results show a considerable discrepancy between expectation and actuality. Not only are participation and knowledge scores negatively correlated but different social variables are relevant to the understanding of each type of score. Before attempting to explain these differences, I summarise the findings of the various statistical tests.

The slight negative correlation between knowledge and participation scores are expressed in Table V/2. This table suggests a number of interesting trends. It shows that slightly less than one third of the sample (29 per cent) have high knowledge scores. In part, this finding may be related to the limited number of responses on which the knowledge scale is based, but sociological factors, which are discussed below, are probably more significant. The table also shows that whereas 84 per cent of the respondents with high participation scores have low knowledge scores, 43 per cent of those with low participation scores have high knowledge scores. Moreover, 60 per cent of the respondents with low knowledge scores have high participation scores, while 71 per cent of those with high knowledge scores have low participation scores. Thus, the negative correlation between participation and knowledge scores is well-defined.

TABLE V/2
KNOWLEDGE AND PARTICIPATION SCORES

Participation Scores	Knowledge Scores	
	High	Low
High	8	41
Low	20	27

$X^2 = 6.9$; $p < .01$. Range of participation scores: Low: 60–79; High: 80–103. Range of knowledge scores: Low: 0–1; High: 2–3.

When multivariant analysis of variance tests are applied to the two scale scores independently, further discrepancies between preliminary hypotheses and actuality are revealed. These tests show that different variables are relevant to the understanding of the two sets of scores (see Table V/3). The variables relevant to participation scores are area, class, house type, and age. These variables produce their effects independently and may be ranged in order of diminishing significance from area and class through house type to age. By contrast, knowledge scores are explained by sex and secondarily by age. The most striking result of

TABLE V/3
MULTIVARIANT ANALYSIS OF VARIANCE RESULTS

Variables Tested	Participation Scores		Knowledge Scores	
		P.		P
Area by Sex by Age	Area	.001	Sex	.001
	Age	.025	Age	.01
Class by Age by Sex	Class	.001	Sex	.025
			Age	.025
Area by Class	Area	.001	Not significant	
	Class	.001		
Class by House type	Class	.001	Not significant	
	House type	.01		
Sex by House type	House type	.001	Sex	.01
Age by House type	House type	.001	Age	.001
	Age	.05		

these data is that the variables of primary significance for one set of scores are irrelevant to the other.

This finding is further refined by *chi*-square analysis of the different variables for the two sets of scores. These tests show that high participation scores are associated with the significant variables in the following ways:

Area: Ussher Town > James Town > Riponsville (P. < .001);
Class: low > high (P. < .001);
House type: Unisexual kin unit > Bisexual kin unit with dependent conjugal family > Bisexual kin unit > Conjugal family unit (P. < .02);
Age: 60+ > 45–59 > 30–44 (P. not significant).

Thus, the values of the variables for high participation scores correspond to the preliminary hypotheses concerning adherence to traditional standards. *Chi*-square tests of the relationship between high knowledge scores and the significant variables disclose the opposite trend. High knowledge is associated with the two variables in the following ways:

Sex: Male > Female (P. .05);
Age: 30–44 > 45–60+ > 15–29 (P. not significant).

In summary, these statistical tests show that different variables explain the two sets of scores and that the values of the relevant variables accord with preliminary hypotheses concerning traditionality for the participation scores but that they do not correspond for knowledge scores.

The statistical analysis may be refined further by an examination of responses to different items within each set of questions. Item analysis not only supports the preceding argument but also discloses illuminating variations within each set of responses. When correlations between participation scores and participation questions are analysed, participation scores are positively correlated with eleven items and are not significantly related to eight items. High participation scores are associated with responses to five religious and six secular items. The former are non-Christian status, knowledge of family god's name, belief in the supernatural powers of twins and healers, and burial of the dead's *exuviae* in the family house. The latter are participation in the traditional political system, use of traditional medicine, non-use of modern mass media, disapproval of intertribal marriage, and lack of non-Ga friends.

The eight items which are not significantly related to participation scores are particularly interesting, for they reflect the continuing relevance of certain traditional beliefs and practices and the generality of a number of other ideas within the Ga community. Three questions pertain to secular matters: most informants perceive Ga culture as similar to other southern Ghanaian cultures but as different from northern Ghanaian and non-Ghanaian cultures; while most people consult senior kinsmen with personal problems, very few consult their spouses; and few people offer any other rationalization of the residential separation of the sexes other than it is a Ga custom.

The five statistically non-significant religious items disclose the persistence of certain religious beliefs and ritual and the prevalence of certain changes in ritual observance. In response to a query about the celebration of the Rite of Feasting (*Hɔmɔwɔ*), 95 per cent of the respondents observed the rite the preceding year and 55 per cent say that the rite was celebrated with a preliminary purificatory rite in their family houses. While these two items related to the persistence of traditional religion, the other three items pertain to changes in ritual performance. The question concerning marriage ritual is applicable to 69 per cent of the respondents; 7 per cent of these married in church, 12 per cent observed the traditional wedding rite, and 81 per cent performed the traditional betrothal ceremony (see Chapter IV). Apart from the traditional wedding rite, the other traditional life crisis ceremony which is infrequently observed is the puberty rite, which had been performed for only 11 per cent of the respondents. A new ceremony which is observed with greater frequency than the church wedding is the afternoon naming rite, which slightly more than half the sample had performed for their first offspring. Thus, although these eight items fail to differentiate respondents with high participation scores from those with low scores, they reflect the generality of various ideas and practices within the contemporary Ga population in Central Accra and support the institutional analyses of the preceding chapters.

The nature and limited number of knowledge questions both permits and requires a slightly different analysis of responses than the participation questions. While it is inappropriate to evaluate responses to participation questions according to a standard of suitability, it is necessary to apply such a standard to replies to knowledge questions. A respondent either is or is not able to explain, fully or partially, the meaning of a knowledge question. Although respondents occasionally give interpretations to questions which do not accord with the interpretations of acknowledged ritual authorities, respondents who do not know the meaning of knowledge questions usually say either that they do not know or that the ritual is 'customary (*Ga kusum*)'. Thus respondents may be grouped in categories based on the number of correct responses (see Table V/4). Although a majority of respondents were able to interpret only one question, twelve were unable to interpret any question, and no one was able to interpret all four.

Three social variables (sex, age, and class) show interesting relationships with knowledge scores. The sexual composition of each category in Table V/4 is especially illuminating: male respondents alone were able to interpret three items; males constitute 57 per cent of those who interpreted two items, 45 per cent of those who could explain one item, and 33 per cent of those who were unable to answer any question appropriately. Although this finding is consistent with the results of the analysis of variance tests of knowledge scores, the distribution of the sexes within the two polar categories is particularly suggestive. The age and class distributions for respondents in the polar categories are also pertinent. While 57 per cent of those who answered three questions are also in the oldest age category and 67 per cent of those who answered none are in the youngest age category, 25 per cent of the respondents who were unable to answer any question appropriately were also over sixty years of age. Whereas 71 per cent of those who answered three questions are in the higher socio-economic category, 75 per cent of those who answered none are also in this category. These findings not only reaffirm the results of the analysis of variance tests, but indicate that different factors must be considered in the explanation of response categories of knowledge and participation questions.

An analysis of responses to each knowledge question reveals both discrepancies between ritual performance and interpretation and variations in the distribution of correct responses to each question. Whereas 80 per cent of the respondents were able to interpret the

TABLE V/4
RESPONSE TO KNOWLEDGE QUESTIONS BY SOCIAL ATTRIBUTES

Attributes	*Correct Responses*			
	0	*1*	*2*	*3*
Area				
Ussher Town	2	25	5	—
James Town	3	17	8	4
Riponsville	7	14	8	3
Sex				
Male	4	25	12	7
Female	8	31	9	—
Age				
15–29	8	13	3	—
30–44	1	13	8	2
45–59	—	16	7	1
60+	3	14	3	4
Class				
I	3	40	11	2
II	9	16	10	5
Household Type				
1	2	2	3	2
2	2	10	7	1
3	6	23	7	4
4	2	21	4	—
N.	12	56	21	7

phrase from the marriage ritual, only 27 per cent were able to interpret the phrase from the naming prayer, 13 per cent the phrase from the final funerary ceremony, and 4 per cent the meaning of the preliminary purificatory rite at the Rite of Feasting. These gross figures can be refined by an examination of the distribution of respondents in terms of ability to explain a number of items (see Table V/5). These data suggest that certain items may be more difficult to interpret than others. The items may be ranged in order of increasing difficulty from marriage ritual, through naming ritual, to funeral ritual, to Rite of Feasting ritual. The data further suggest that the probability of interpreting a number of items corresponds to the ability to explicate difficult questions. Thus, the question relating to marriage ritual was

TABLE V/5
DISTRIBUTION OF RESPONDENTS BY ITEMS

Correct Interpretation	Question Concerning Ritual of			
	Marriage	Naming	Funeral	Rite of Feasting
	%	%	%	%
This item only	65	15	17	—
This item and one other item	27	66	33	—
This item and two other items	8	19	50	(100)*
Total	100	100	100	100
N.	77	26	12	4

*Base less than ten cases.

answered correctly with greatest frequency, but the majority of those who interpreted the question were only able to answer that item. By contrast, everyone who interpreted the question concerning the Rite of Feasting ritual could interpret two other items. The responses to the item concerning the meaning of the preliminary purificatory ritual at the Rite of Feasting are relevant to the problem of the discrepancy between ritual performance and the interpretation of ritual. Women perform this rite, but only men were able to interpret it. Moreover, while 55 per cent of the respondents celebrated the Rite of Feasting with this preliminary rite, only 4 per cent were able to interpret it.

These statistical results involve two major interpretative problems. The first is an explanation of the difference between the values of the significant variables for the two types of scores. The second is an evaluation of the implications of these differences to the general problem of cultural continuity and change within the Ga population of Central Accra. Since these issues are fairly complex, the tentative nature of the explanatory formulations which I offer should be appreciated.

The statistical analysis has shown that participation and knowledge scores may be attributed to different variables and that whereas the values of the relevant variables of the high participation scores accord with preliminary hypotheses concerning traditionality and social variables, the values of the appropriate variables for high knowledge scores do not. High participation scores are associated equally with residential area and socio-economic status and to a lesser extent with household type and age. The statistical analysis also shows that the interaction between these variables is not significant or that the variables produce their effects independently. Persons with high participation scores, therefore, are predominantly of lower socio-economic status and are more likely to be living in Ussher Town than in the other areas and in James Town than in Riponsville; further, they are usually older people living in traditionally structured household units.

Since the salient variables are residential area and socio-economic status, the explanation for high participation scores may be attributed to the inability of individuals to make effective use of modernizing ideas and lack of exposure to such ideas. Typically, the person with a high participation score has received a minimal amount of western education and, therefore, is unable to compete for employment within the modern occupational system; he lives in a neighbourhood which not only is populated predominantly by his fellow-tribesmen but has been relatively stable in its composition for many years, and in which, therefore, interpersonal relationships are dominated by personal norms. These factors are reinforced by his membership in a household which is structured according to traditional principles and by his age, for he came to maturity before the Second World War. Although he may be aware of alternative ideas and modernizing trends, his effective use of them is severely limited by his lack of requisite skills and by his membership in a community which sanctions traditional norms for behaviour.

By contrast, high knowledge scores are determined first by sex and secondarily by age. High knowledge scores are associated unequivocally with masculinity. This association, irrespective of any other consideration, indicates that its explanation is to be found in some factor which is operative in both traditional and modern social systems. In traditional Ga society, men are considered rational thinkers whereas women are conceptualized as irrational people (see Chapter IV). This concept underlies the principles of male superordination which is expressed in traditional society in various ways and which is also appropriate to an understanding of industrial society. It is inappropriate to argue that men know the meaning of ritual because they perform it, for two of the four knowledge questions involve ritual performed by women. Moreover, one of the rites which women perform could only be interpreted by male respondents.

Rather, these data suggest that the modernization process may reinforce traditional principles. While class is not a significant variable for knowledge scores *per se*, an examination of high knowledge scores in terms of this variable is illuminating. Although the proportion of persons of lower socio-economic status with high knowledge scores is the same for both sexes, the proportion of persons of higher social status with similar scores differs by sex.[6] Moreover, this difference is greater than the difference between the proportion of high knowledge scores for persons of the same sex in different social class statuses, for while the largest proportion of women with high knowledge scores are of lower class status, the largest proportion of men with similar scores are of higher class status. These data imply that the traditional concept of men as rational thinkers is reinforced by the modernization process. The explanation for this reinforcement may be attributed partly to the value which Western education places on speculative thought and partly to the heightened awareness of ethnic values which interaction with persons who do not share the same basic system of ideas may involve.[7]

Such an argument is supported by the trend in the age categories associated with high knowledge scores. The highest proportion of high-knowledge respondents is in the 30—44 age category, while the medial proportion of respondents is in the two oldest age categories, and the lowest proportion in the 15—29 age category. The explanation for the high proportion of 30—44 years and the low proportion of 15—29 years is related to responsibility for the performance of ritual; many of the latter are unmarried young people who consequently have not been directly involved in marital ritual for themselves or birth ritual for their children, nor are they likely to have had responsibility for the performance of funerary rites. The explanation for the differences between the 30—44 age category and the older age categories, however, probably is attributable to reinforcement within the modernization context, which is also consistent with the negative correlation between knowledge and participation scores.

The second analytical problem to be considered is the relationship of these findings to the problem of cultural continuity and change within the Ga community of Central Accra. These data show that cultural continuity within the urban context is possible for individuals at the level of belief and behaviour and at the level of interpretative understanding of traditional customs. They also indicate that the two levels of traditionality vary independently. They further imply that involvement with traditional culture at the level of ideas and behaviour is constrained by socio-economic and demographic factors to a greater extent than at the level of interpretative understanding of culture. Social change factors, therefore, operate more explicitly at the former level than at the latter level.

I suggest that the interpretative level of understanding relates to the concept of male superordination which is relevant to both traditional and modern society. Thus high knowledge scores are related ambiguously to considerations of either social continuity or social change, except in that persons with higher socio-economic status are freer to opt whether or not to concern themselves with aspects of traditional society. Nevertheless, it should be noted that the proportion of respondents with high knowledge scores is fairly low (29 per cent), which is consistent with the expectation that in any society the proportion of persons who concern themselves with philosophical issues is relatively small.[8] Finally, on the basis of these admittedly limited data, it is clear that cultural continuity at the individual level of analysis is present within the Ga community of Central Accra; this process is facilitated by the stability and the long-established nature of the Ga population in Accra.

REFERENCES

1. See Appendix for questions and response coding.
2. The ninety-six respondents were selected from 396 informants in the household survey which is discussed in Chapter III. Selection was based on neighbourhood, sex, and age, because initially the other variables were not ascertainable.
3. The three residential areas were selected, because I thought that the proportion of Ga varied significantly between areas. I anticipated that the highest concentration of Ga would be found in Ussher Town, the lowest in Riponsville, and that James Town would constitute a medial area. My hypothesis was based on temporal and demographic considerations. Although Ussher Town and James Town are both old areas of Ga settlement, not only is the former considered to be the community which was settled first, but the latter is the area in which many immigrant fishermen and seamen reside. Riponsville began to develop as a residential area during the first quarter of this century. Table V/6, based on unpublished census data which were inaccessible until the conclusion of the survey, shows that the overall difference in the concentration of Ga in the three residential areas is not as high as had been anticipated. There is, however, a marked difference in the sex distribution. The proportion of Ga women follows the anticipated trend for the areas, while that of Ga men does not. Although the reasons for this difference are not known, the large proportion of single men from Liberia and western Ghana in James Town probably accounts for the low proportion of Ga men in that area. This explanation is supported by the fact that the Ga sex ratio is approximately the same for each of the residental areas. In each area the number of women exceeds that of men. Ga women constitute 58 per cent of the Ga population in both Ussher Town and James Town, 57 per cent in Riponsville, and 56 per cent in Central Accra. Thus although the ethnic

TABLE V/6
PROPORTION OF GA IN EACH RESEARCH AREA

Area	Total	Male	Female
Ussher Town	79	72	82
James Town	54	40	72
Riponsville	51	47	56

differences between the three research areas are slightly ambiguous, the anticipated trend is present.

Variations in the demographic attributes of the three research areas are negligible in certain respects and significant in others. Corresponding to the high proportion of Accra-born Ga in each area is the similarity in the sex ratios and balanced age profiles in the three residential areas. Analysis of the educational and occupational statistics for the areas (see Table V/7), however, shows important socio-economic differences between the three communities. The socio-economic differences range from low to high in the order in which I anticipated that ethnic homogeneity would range. Thus, Ussher Town occupied the lowest position on the socio-economic scale, James Town the medial, and Riponsville, the highest. Further, a large difference exists between the socio-economic status of men and women within the same area. The higher socio-economic status of men is consistent with the greater educational opportunities available to men. In summary, the Ga population in the three residential areas of Central Accra is differentiated according to socio-economic variables and to a lesser extent in terms of ethnic homogeneity.

TABLE V/7
SOCIO-ECONOMIC DIFFERENCES AMONG GA IN CENTRAL ACCRA

Item	Ussher Town		James Town		Riponsville	
	Male	*Female*	*Male*	*Female*	*Male*	*Female*
	%	%	%	%	%	%
Occupation						
Administrative,						
Professional	4	1	9	1	10	2
Clerical	11	2	19	4	25	6
Sales	3	88	5	85	5	77
Fishing, Farming	41	–	21	–	8	2
Labor	41	9	46	10	52	13
Education (Past						
and Present)						
Never	42	81	31	77	20	69
Primary	7	5	8	5	7	8
Middle	44	13	48	15	58	22
Secondary or More	7	1	13	3	15	3
Total	100	100	100	100	100	100

4. While it is possible for a person with a considerable amount of Western education to have a traditional occupation, the converse is impossible. An examination of the unpublished Central Accra census data for 1960, for example, shows that while the majority of Ga fishermen have never attended school, a number of fishermen have

completed middle school. In such cases, an individual's current occupation would assume precedence in assigning socio-economic status.

5. See Chapter III.

6. Women with high knowledge scores: Class I: 30 per cent; Class II: 20 per cent. Men with high knowledge scores: Class I: 30 per cent; Class II: 44 per cent.

7. e.g. Jean Rouch's concept of 'supertribalism'. (J. Rouch, 'Migrations au Ghana', *Journal de la Société des Africanistes* 26, 1956, pp. 163—4.

8. See P. Radin, *Primitive Man as a Philosopher*, New York, 1927, pp. 5, 229—91 and M. Griaule, 'Le Savior des Dogon', *Journal de la Société des Africanistes 22*, 1952, pp. 27—42.

CHAPTER VI

CONCLUSION

In this study my central concern has been continuity and change in the kinship system of the Ga community of Central Accra, who constitute a stable West African urban population. Although my analysis focuses on the persistence of traditional kinship ideas and institutions, I also discuss certain processes of social change and the underlying factors which explain both social continuity and change. I consider that ultimately social continuity within the Ga community depends upon demographic and socio-economic considerations. While the stability and perpetuity of the population provide the context within which traditional standards may persist, the preponderance of members of unskilled and traditional occupational categories within the population limits the extent to which alternative modernizing ideas and values may be effectively utilized. The modernization process is the main factor accounting for social change. Analysis of the relationship between ideas and institutional change suggests that institutional change may result from emphasising alternative principles within the traditional social system or assimilating new social concepts which either may replace or may reinforce certain traditional social ideas. Although the modernization process leads to new bases of socio-economic differentiation within the community, my analysis suggests that such differentiations are pertinent to certain types of social continuity and irrelevant to others. Social continuity at the level of belief and practice appears to be closely correlated with lower or more traditional socio-economic status, whereas social continuity at the level of interpretative understanding of traditional ideas seems to be unrelated to socio-economic consider- ations or factors of change.

The point of departure in this study is an analysis of Ga kinship conceptions and institutions. An examination of the discrepancies between the ideal and actual Ga residential system in Central Accra shows that while traditional ideas are pertinent to an understanding of contemporary Ga domestic units, certain modifications have been introduced. Although these modifications constitute a response to ideas and pressures which derive from the modernization process, they are explicable in terms of certain alternative ideas and principles which are operative within the traditional system, rather than in terms of the assimilation of new or unrelated concepts.

The significance of blood kinship for organizing social groups within the contemporary Ga social system is reflected in the cycle of life crisis ceremonies. These ceremonies have adjusted to the modernization process by adapting to express new ideas of association and prestige. Although certain ceremonies are no longer observed and others have been introduced, the present set of ceremonies is universally observed and expresses the continuing relevance of blood kinship bonds throughout the Ga community in Central Accra.

Modernization has led to new bases of social differentiation within the Ga community of Central Accra. It emerged that participation in the traditional social system at the level of belief and behaviour is determined primarily by socio-economic status. Thus, lower class status is associated with high participation in the traditional social system and higher class status with low participation. Active participation in the traditional social system, however, is not associated with interpretative understanding of traditional custom. Rather, such information is associated with sexual differentiation, in such a way that masculinity and greater knowledge are associated. I have suggested that this finding can be explained, on the one hand, by certain traditional ideas concerning differences between the sexes in Ga society and, on the other hand, by the limited number of persons in any society who are concerned with epistemological problems.

The principal conclusion of this case study of Ga kinship in Central Accra is that aspects of the traditional social system which are not directly associated with the industrial complex may persist within African urban units. Such persistence is undoubtedly related to the stable continuity of the urban population. The social systems of migrant townsmen, therefore, are likely to be quite different from those of traditional townsmen. Within stable core populations, variations in adherence to the traditional social system may be expected. These variations will be related partially but not exclusively to socio-economic considerations. To the extent that this conclusion is based on limited data pertaining to people living in a restricted area under quite similar conditions, it might be reexamined profitably among Ga living in the suburbs of Accra, who include a greater socio-economic range, and among the core population of another urban centre, such as the Yoruba in Lagos, Nigeria.

QUESTIONS AND UNSCALED RESPONSE CODING FOR CULTURAL SURVEY

A. Participation Questions

1. If you had to borrow money from whom would you borrow it?
1. Bank; 2. Money-lender; 3. Kinsman.

2. What do you think about a Ga person marrying a non-Ga?
1. Approve; 2. Disapprove.

3. Do you have any non-Ga friends? 1. Yes; 2. No.

4. Of the following which are the most/least like Ga: Ashanti, Fanti, Ewe, Yoruba, Dagomba, Hausa? 1. All like Ga; 2. Southern Ghanaians like Ga; Northern Ghanaians and Nigerians unlike Ga; 3. None like Ga.

5. Imagine that your father, mother, spouse, brother, sister, son and daughter are all living and adult. If you had a personal problem with whom would you discuss it first? 1. Spouse; 2. Kin same or junior generation; 3. Kin senior generation.

6. What kind of ceremony was performed when you were married for the first time? 1. Church wedding; 2. Betrothal ceremony; 3. Traditional wedding ceremony.

7. When your mother/father died, where were the sponge, nails, and hair buried? 1. Not removed from corpse; 2. In house.

8. How did you celebrate the Rite of Feasting last year? 1. Not celebrated; 2. Celebrated; 3. Celebrated and preceded by purificatory rite (*akpade*).

9. If you were sick to whom would you go to be cured? 1. Doctor; 2. Doctor and healer; 3. Healer.

10. When I talk to healers about their work, they tell me that often their patients go to Korle Bu Hospital before they come to them. Do you think that sometimes healers can cure people when western medicine fails? 1. Yes; 2. No.

11. Why do Ga women often live in separate houses from Ga men? 1. Poverty; 2. Custom; 3. Women are ritually impure.

12. Do you believe that twins have greater powers than other people? 1. No; 2. Yes.

13. What does it mean if you dream that an animal such as a cow or a lion is chasing you? If you had such a dream what would you do? 1. No meaning and do nothing; 2. Supernatural being but do nothing; 3. Supernatural being and do something.

14. What is the name of your family god? 1. Do not know; 2. Know.

15. Are you a Christian? When did you last go to church? 1. Active Christian (within last month); 2. Passive Christian; 3. Non-Christian.

16. Do you plan to go to the presentation of the new Ga paramount chief at *Amuginaa*? Did you vote in the last national election? 1. Voted and do not plan to go to *Amuginaa*; 2. Voted and plan to go; 3. Neither voted nor plan to go.

17. How often do you listen to the radio? How often do you go to the cinema? 1. Radio daily and cinema within last month; 2. Radio occasionally and cinema occasionally; 3. Never listen to radio and never been to cinema.

18. Was puberty rite performed for you? 1. Yes; 2. No.

19. Did you celebrate the birth of your first child with an afternoon naming rite? 1. Yes; 2. No.

B. Knowledge Questions

What is the meaning of:

1. 'May our stools be thicker, may our brooms be thicker' in the naming prayer? 1. Do not know; 2. May the males in the family increase; 3. May the females in the family increase.

2. 'May we wade in blood' from the marriage ceremony? 1. Do not know; 2. May children be born.

3. 'Today you have crossed the river' from the funeral ceremony? 1. Do not know; 2. You have assumed the status of ancestral shade.

4. The *akpade* rite performed before the Rite of Feasting? 1. Do not know; 2. Purification of the house of any evil which may have entered it during the year.

GA HEALERS AND PATIENTS

Everywhere people necessarily experience tensions in their lives arising from various biosocial sources and having diverse social and physiological consequences. The recent literature on contemporary African society indicates the variety of institutional forms from curing cult to prophetic church through which urban and rural folk attempt to explain and to resolve such significant personal issues as reproductive disorders, marital conflicts, and economic insecurities. In this appendix I report the results of an attempt to gain some insight into the personal concerns of Central Accra dwellers as revealed in the medical practice of Ga healers (*tsofatsę*, lit., tree root owner or medicine owner). Through weekly interviews with six professional healers I gained some information about the social attributes, complaints, diagnoses, and therapy of 131 people treated by these medical practitioners during three months in 1965.

The healers who lived and worked in Central Accra and its environs were enterprising older Ga men representing quite diverse social backgrounds and experiences. Some spoke only Ga; others spoke and wrote English fluently. Some were members of Christian churches; others adhered to traditional religious cults, and one was a Muslim. Earlier in their lives they had pursued various occupations including those of school teacher, cloth designer, soldier, Christian evangelist, and fisherman. As professional healers they appeared to enjoy varying material success but to share a lively interest in acquiring new therapeutic ideas and information.

Their patients' social attributes were equally diverse. Patients included Ga (87 or 66 per cent) and non-Ga, males (55 or 42 per cent) and females, adults (97 or 74 per cent) and children. Of the 103 patients whose religious affiliations are known, the vast majority (92 or 89 per cent) were Christian, two were Muslims, and the remainder adhered to traditional cults. While the occupations of adults ranged from petty trader and fisherman through skilled worker and nurse to university student and lawyer, more adult patients (66 or 68 per cent) fell into the lower socio-economic category (described in Chapter V) than into the higher class category (31 or 32 per cent).

Healers conversing.

On the advice of relatives or friends and sometimes after resorting unsuccessfully to western medicine (29 cases or 22 per cent), patients came to healers with both physical ailments (100 or 76 per cent) and social concerns (31 or 24 per cent). Fully one quarter of the physical complaints were concerned with sexual and reproductive disorders; eighteen women came to healers about barrenness, irregular menses, or venereal disease, while seven men consulted healers about impotency or venereal disease. The next largest category of physical complaints was mental illness (13) followed by skin diseases (4) and convulsions (4). The remaining physical complaints involved one or two cases of ailments such as constipation, malaria, leprosy, piles, and heart disease.

The social concerns about which patients consulted healers included protective medicine against evil or for success (10), assistance in finding a job or in gaining a promotion (5), help in retrieving an errant lover or spouse (5), solutions to studying problems (3), and aid in finding 'disappearing' money (3). All these social concerns are particularly germane to people coping with a relatively anonymous and competitive social milieu in which success depends on western educational achievement and/or monetary wealth.

The next phase in the therapeutic process after the initial complaint of the patient is the healer's diagnosis. As in traditional Ga society, contemporary healers utilize both physical and spiritual concepts in diagnosing and treating their patients' complaints. Of the 131 patients' complaints, healers judged that 66 (50 per cent) had supernatural causes such as 'evil forces' (11), witchcraft or sorcery (47), or a curse (2). Thus, of the 100 physical complaints, healers determined that fifty-one had supernatural causes, forty-eight purely physical origins, and one a psychological source. By contrast, of the thirty-one social concerns, healers decided that fifteen had supernatural causes, two psychological origins, and one a physical source, while such an original cause was irrelevant in thirteen cases. Ga healers believe that diseases which are supernaturally induced are more difficult to cure than purely physical diseases and that supernaturally caused ailments cannot be treated by western medicine (see Chapter V).

Although patients often offer explanations of the causes of their complaints, healers as frequently disagree with their patients' interpretations, though they may prefer not to reveal their conflicting diagnosis. For example, one healer described a girl who was brought to him in a 'nearly imbecilic state'; her relatives claimed that some enemy had cast a spell over her, but the healer determined that the girl was suffering from malnutrition. In another instance, a child suffered from convulsions that the healer determined were caused by witchcraft; the child's twin had just died from similarly induced convulsions, but the child's Muslim father, who did not believe in witches, failed to follow the healer's advice about treating the dead child; the father, however, agreed to do what the healer suggested for the second. In a third case, a barren woman believed that her co-wife had bewitched her, but the healer determined that her barrenness had a physical cause; he, however, did not tell the woman of his opinion, as he believed that she would not take the medicine that he prescribed for physical reasons.

Certain healers treat patients only on an out-patient basis, others take in-patients as well as out-patients. Two of the six healers whom I know had 'villages' outside the city, where they treated long-term illnesses; at least two had rooms in their Accra houses reserved for the hospitalization of patients, and two saw only out-patients.

In treating patients healers can choose among several forms of therapy including dream analysis, medicinal injections, internal and external medications, fasting, prayer, sacrifice, and incense burning. Although a healer may specialize in some particular therapeutic procedure, such as a unique form of pictorial writing developed by one healer, it is quite unusual for a healer to use only one form of therapy to treat a particular case. Thus, in only 42 of 131 cases (32 per cent) was only one form of therapy used. Two popular therapeutic combinations are (1) some internal medication, a purificatory bath, and some other form of therapy such as prayer, fasting, or sacrifice, and (2) both external and internal medications and incense burining or having an enema. Despite the diversity of healing techniques and their combinations, the frequency of their use differed. Among the 131 cases, the most popular form of therapy was some internal medication (63 per cent), followed by external medication (29 per cent), purificatory bathing (28 per cent), massaging (11 per cent), prayer (11 per cent), and enemas (10 per cent). In order to understand the choice of therapy in a particular case, however, it is necessary to consider both the patient's initial complaint and the healer's diagnosis of its cause.

An analysis of patients' complaints in terms of therapy shows a different rank ordering in the popularity of therapeutic forms for physical and social complaints. For the 100 physical complaints, the four most frequently used forms of therapy were internal medication (79 per cent), external medication (27 per cent), purificatory bathing (25 per cent), and massage (15 per cent). By contrast the four most popular techniques for dealing with thirty-one social complaints were purificatory bathing (42 per cent), external medication (38 per cent), incense burning (19 per cent), and prayer (13 per cent). This analysis suggests the relative importance of physical therapeutic techniques for physical complaints and mystical procedures for social concerns.

This correspondence between form of complaint and form of therapy is reinforced by an examination of the relationship between diagnosis and treatment. For the forty-eight cases diagnosed as physically caused, the four most popular treatments were internal medication (85 per cent), external medication (27 per cent), enema (25 per cent), and massage (21 per cent). The forms of therapy for sixty-six cases diagnosed as supernaturally caused, irrespective of the nature of the initial complaint, ranged from internal medication (56 per cent), through purificatory bathing (39 per cent) and external medication (27 per cent), to prayer (17 per cent). Although the association between physical diagnoses and physical forms of therapy is clear, the relationship between supernatural diagnoses and mystical forms of therapy is more ambiguous.

Examination of the circumstances in which seven popular forms of therapy are used clarifies certain aspects of the relationship between complaint, diagnosis, and therapeutic form (see Table B/1). Of the eighty-two cases treated with internal medication, 96 per cent were physical complaints but only 50 per cent were diagnosed as physical in origin. Of the thirty-nine cases treated with external medication, 69 per cent were physical complaints, but 33 per cent were considered to be physically caused and 46 per cent to be supernaturally caused, while 21 per cent had some other origin. Of the thirty-eight cases treated with purificatory bathing, 66 per cent were both physical complaints and supernatural in origin, but only 17 per cent were diagnosed as physically caused. Of the fifteen cases treated with massage, all were physical complaints and 67 per cent were diagnosed as physically caused. Of the fifteen cases involving treatment by prayer, 80 per cent concerned both physical complaints and supernatural diagnoses. Of the thirteen cases treated with enemas, all were physical complaints and 92 per cent were diagnosed as physically caused. Finally, of the eight cases treated with purification through incense burning, 75 per cent originated from social complaints and were diagnosed as supernatural in origin. This review of therapeutic forms suggests that massage and enema are used as therapy for physical complaints with physical causes, whereas internal and external medications are used for physical complaints irrespective of their cause; mystical forms of therapy such as special baths and prayers are used primarily for physical complaints with supernatural causes. In treating social complaints, however, non-physical forms of therapy are especially important. Thus, there is a general – albeit imperfect – association between forms of complaint, diagnoses, and treatment.

TABLE B/1
THERAPY, COMPLAINT, AND CAUSE OF COMPLAINT

Form of Therapy	Physical complaint (N: 100)			Social complaint (N: 31)	
	Physical Cause (N: 48)	Supernatural Cause (N: 51)	Other Cause (N: 1)	Supernatural Cause (N: 13)	Other (N: 16)
Internal medication (N: 82)	41	37	1	–	3
External medication (N: 39)	13	13	1	5	7
Purificatory bath (N: 38)	6	19	–	7	6
Massage (N: 15)	10	5	–	–	–
Prayer (N: 15)	1	11	–	1	3
Enema (N: 13)	12	1	–	–	–
Incense burning (N: 8)	–	1	1	5	1

The following cases illustrate the dynamic operation of some of these considerations:

A wealthy man came to a healer with bad skin sores. The healer determined that this physical ailment was caused by another poorer man who was involved in a land dispute with the patient. Initially the land was sold to the poor man who feared that the patient would use bribery to get the land, so he bewitched the patient.

The healer said that the patient had been sick for about six months and that before coming to him had gone to Korle Bu Hospital and to Togo for treatment.

The healer treated the patient by boiling medicine made from some powdered root. The patient's hands were put into the medicine; later he bathed in this medicated water with a special soap; and he placed powder on his sores. He was said to have been cured in seven weeks.

An impotent man came to a healer to be cured. The patient had slept with a woman whose husband had put a 'medicine' on her that would cause any man who slept with her to become impotent.

The healer bought a cock, killed it, removed its testicles, reduced them to a powder, and 'vaccinated' the patient's waist and knees with the powder to stop the 'power' of the medicine. The healer also gave the patient 'medicine' to drink.

A private contractor who wanted a government contract came to a healer for assistance. The healer advised him to take a special bath consisting of leaves and water from a distant waterfall every three days over a three-week period. Before going to speak to the official from whom he wanted the contract, the contractor was advised to put on a scented oil.

The healer said that the contractor succeeded in gaining the desired contract.

A young policeman who was involved in an extortion case was jailed without bail. The policeman's relatives came to a healer to pray that he might be released on bail. Their prayers were answered after five days of prayer.

When the case came to trial, the policeman stayed with the healer, who prayed that the witnesses' testimony would be confused; the policeman was acquitted and reinstated in his job on the police force. The healer, however, advised him to resign his position.

After the man resigned from the police force, the healer prayed that he would find a new job. The young man succeeded in getting a job with the agricultural department. Shortly afterwards he had an opportunity to go abroad for further study.

A trader came to a healer, because she was unsuccessful in her business and thought that she had been bewitched The healer gave her a soap with which to bathe and incense to burn; he also told her to give alms, as from her conversation he had found her to be selfish rather than unsuccessful.

A clerk who forged a GCE certificate to get a job was discovered and jailed. A relative of his wife put up his bail and he was released. Before his case came to trial, the man came to a healer for assistance. The healer prayed on behalf of the man, and he ultimately determined that the man would be fined £50 rather than imprisoned.

In this limited analysis of aspects of the practice of six Ga healers in Central Accra, I have tried to show how some contemporary urban dwellers attempt to cope with important personal problems through the patient-healer relationship. As I have noted, both healers and patients are diverse in their social attributes. Patients approach healers with a variety of physical and social concerns which receive diverse explanations and treatments from healers. Both patients and healers, however, share certain basic assumptions about the possibilities of supernatural forces operating in human affairs as both causative and therapeutic factors. Through relationships with healers, patients attempt to maximize predictability in lives played within the context of a competitive urban milieu, whether the immediate issue over which they seek both explanatory and physical control be promotion in a job or the birth of a child.

URBAN ETHNOGRAPHIC FIELDWORK

Traditionally the role of ethnographer implied not only certain methods of inquiry but a locus of inquiry in small-scale societies of the non-Western world. Increasingly ethnographic modes of inquiry, especially participant observation and unstructured interviews with key informants, are used in diverse societal contexts throughout the world. Moreover, the ethnographer researching in urban contexts has had to add certain quantitative techniques to his methodological tool chest. An urban ethnographer's selection of research procedures depends partly on the topic of inquiry and partly upon certain personal and situational constraints. Nevertheless, a researcher's identification as urban ethnographer probably necessitates some reliance upon the traditional ethnographic technique of lengthy unstructured interviews involving long-term multiplex relationships with certain 'key informants'.

The contractual relationship between ethnographer and informant is based upon the reciprocal exchange of services. Although the initiation of the relationship usually depends upon the ethnographer, its development and continuity depends upon the perceptions of both parties either of whom may terminate or alter the relationship. Central to the continuity of the ethnographer-informant relationship is the development of mutual trust and satisfaction deriving both from the ethnographer's perception of the informant's services and demands and from the informant's perception of the ethnographer's demands and rewards. From the ethnographer's perspective, the informant must possess a number of attributes: reliability, knowledge, and congeniality. The connotations of reliability may include internally consistent and not obviously distorted information, willingness to admit limits of knowledge, and predictable availability to interact with the ethnographer. Apart from reliability, the ethnographer is concerned that his informant is knowledgeable about the topics of interest to the researcher in such a way that each interaction meaningfully increases the ethnographer's knowledge. Another attribute which may significantly influence both parties' perceptions of the relationship is temperamental congeniality. The continuity of the ethnographer-informant relationship depends upon mutual trust and interest in the relationship. As such relationships continue over time, they necessarily encounter certain critical situations, the outcomes of which determine the relationships' future. As a consequence of a particular critical situation, the relationship may be terminated or variously transformed.

Within the context of the ethnographer-informant relationship, the possible dimensions of the informant's role are multiplex. The informant guides the ethnographer not only by conveying information but often by providing access to other sources of information. He censors information by consciously restricting the information available to the ethnographer. He mediates information, in that his interpretation influences the ethnographer's understanding of an issue. He may act as an intermediary between the ethnographer and other persons – to protect the interests of either the ethnographer or the others. In the ethnographer-informant relationship, the quality and multiplexity of the informant's role are best connoted by 'guardian' and that of the ethnographer by 'innocent'.

In this appendix I explore aspects of my experience of the innocent-guardian relationship in the Ga community of Central Accra in 1964–5 and in 1968. My first research venture – reported in this book – was concerned with attempting to understand aspects of social continuity and change within this long-established community of urban folk. My inquiry involved the partial exploration of a variety of topics ranging from traditional social, religious, and political institutions to new voluntary associations and leisure activities and the utilization of diverse research methods including household and cultural surveys, participant observation, unstructured interviews, and archival research. My second study was limited to the investigation of one traditional religious cult and involved solely participant observation and unstructured interviews.

Looking back through avowedly nostalgic glasses to my field experiences in Central Accra, my relationships with three individuals stand out for their ethnographic and personal richness. Each relationship originated during my first field trip and was renewed during my second; each underwent certain transformations resulting from crises specific to that relationship; each relationship involved a distinctive personality who fulfilled the essential criteria of informed, reliable, and congenial guardian to this innocent.

The Innocent

An ethnographer enters the field armed not only with a topic of inquiry but with certain personal and situational constraints affecting his role performance. My most obvious personal constraints included temperament, familial obligations, and linguistic incompetence. Temperamentally reserved, I found survey research necessitating the establishment of fleeting relationships 'on the doorstep' difficult as well as time-consuming. For example, the household survey conducted by myself and one research assistant dragged on from early December 1964 until mid-July 1965, involving 246 house visits to interview 396 adults. I find the traditional ethnographic techniques of participant observation and unstructured interview more rewarding. Not surprisingly, therefore, my second field experience in Accra involved only the utilization of these techniques.

Another personal constraint affecting my ethnographic role was my maternal role. Two babies (7 months, 21 months) in 1964 and three small children (5 years, 4 years, and 2 years) in 1968 accompanied my husband and me to Ghana. The role of mother-surrogate was fulfilled by a succession of Ghanaian nannies in 1964–5 and by an American college student in 1968. Wishing to spend time with my children and to relieve my mother-surrogates necessarily restricted the amount of time available for research. I therefore arranged to spend two hours in the middle of the day at home during my first research venture and two days a week with the children during my second. Leafing through my field diary, I find references to nights spent in the university hospital and mornings spent in the clinic waiting to see a doctor with a sick child. In the middle of my second research trip, one child's illness made me seriously consider abandoning the Ghanaian field for American medical services.

Within the research situation itself, a third personal constraint was the linguistic barrier between me and many Ga informants. Although I spent a considerable part of my early weeks in Accra learning the Ga language, my linguistic incompetence necessitated the use of interpreters with non-English-speaking Ga. Obvious consequences of working through interpreters include the interpreter's conscious censorship and unconscious distortion of information. To minimize these effects, in the latter part of my first field experience and throughout the second I tape recorded all interviews and ritual events. The tapes, which a research assistant transcribed and translated, were valuable for both substantive content and information about characteristic idiosyncratic distortions of individuals acting as linguistic intermediaries between Ga informants and American ethnographer.

Apart from such personal predilections, role-conflicts, and incompetences, a number of related situational constraints affected my role as ethnographer. These included living eight miles outside Central Accra at the university — an arrangement necessitated by my conjugal and maternal commitments. As a commuting ethnographer with erratic means of transportation into field, my potential involvement in the community was severely restricted and my dependence upon predictably available informants increased. Such dependence was enhanced by the urban nature of the field situation itself, by the relatively brief research periods (10 months in 1964–5 and 3 months in 1968), and by financial restraints prohibiting the extensive employment of research assistants. Situational and personal factors, therefore, interacted to produce an 'innocent' for whom relationships with 'guardians' would be particularly congenial and ethnographically rewarding.

The Guardians

Finding a potential guardian depends upon the ethnographer's research interests and situational factors ranging from relationships established in other contexts to chance encounters in the field. Although each guardian later described was found in a different way, additional guardians were found in other ways: our house steward introduced me to the girl who acted as research assistant in 1964 and 1968; American friends living in Accra arranged the intial meeting with another important guardian in 1964–5. Moreover, not all potential guardians whom the ethnographer encountered became guardians. Looking through my field diary I have found several potential guardians with whom the innocent-guardian relationship never developed. The curtailment of such relationships was initiated sometimes by the innocent and at other times by the potential guardian. The guardians described are ones with whom my relationship was richly diverse in content and extensive in time.

Nii Kofi: Aristocratic Ethnographer

Nii Kofi was the only guardian whom I met through university relationships. Throughout his career as a clerk in the civil service, Nii Kofi's avocation had been ethnography. Not only had he read much of the pre-Second World War ethnographic literature in English, but he had been recording – and occasionally publishing – ethnographic information on his culture for thirty years. His reputation as an authoritative ethnographer was appreciated throughout the Ga community and he had assisted several university faculty members in their research on Ga society. Through two of these investigators, I learned of Nii Kofi and where I might find him.

In temperament and status, Nii Kofi was a Ga aristocrat. Through his paternal grandmother he was linked to one of the royal houses of the Ga paramount stool. Within the Ga royal family council he played an influential role in the selection of a new chief in 1964. Through both his traditional status and his ethnographic inquiry, he had ready access to leading members of the Ga traditional political and religious élite in Central Accra. Nii Kofi was regarded by others and by himself as an authority on appropriate traditional behaviour and he was outspokenly critical of deviations from appropriate form. Nevertheless, while insistent on appropriate formal behaviour, Nii Kofi had a very courteous, dignified, and genially warm manner with all whom he encountered, which facilitated the establishment of mutually respectful and co-operative relationships.

Superficially warm and open, Nii Kofi was an intensely private person. Although I came to know — in bits and pieces — a considerable amount about the external contours of his life, he courteously and repeatedly declined to record his autobiography. Often he presented his personal reservations about disclosing information in terms of others' perceptions.

When I met Nii Kofi in 1964, he was elderly and physically frail but vigorous mentally. Following an accident the preceding year, he had moved from his own house on the outskirts of Accra to his senior wife's house, while awaiting the completion of his son's house nearby. There he spent his days engaged in ethnographic writing, newspaper reading, receiving the visits of kinsfolk, and acting occasionally as babysitter for his working daughters' and tenants' children. He left the house to attend meetings of the royal family council and the Ga society, to worship at the Anglican cathedral, to visit his sisters and other wives in Accra, to act as consultant at the Ghana Bureau of Languages, to confer with the head of the royal council, and so on. Considering his physical frailty, which made walking slow and difficult, he led an extremely active life, while accepting with graceful dignity the inevitability of physical death, sustained by a belief in spiritual immortality.

My introduction to Nii Kofi occurred during my second week in Accra in 1964. On that occasion I explained my referral to him, my status as a predoctoral candidate, my interest in understanding Ga society and culture, and requested his assistance in my inquiry. We arranged to meet for an interview the following week. When I arrived for our first interview, I found on the table beside Nii Kofi's chair a large sheet of paper on which he requested that I write my name and my plan of study. The two-hour interview that afternoon initiated an interaction pattern maintained until my departure ten months later· two afternoons each week we met to discuss aspects of the Ga social system. As time went on, a recurrent interview pattern emerged: first, a report of events of mutual interest occurring in both our lives since the preceding meeting; second, a *postmortem* on some event which we had observed together; third, an open-ended discussion of some topic, sometimes stimulated by a paper which he had lent me. During the ten months, the general sequence of topics discussed was social units, life crisis ritual, political institutions, and religious institutions.

Although as the innocent I initiated interaction with Nii Kofi, he as the guardian clearly defined his perception of our relationship at our first interview. By requesting that I write the plan of inquiry, by criticising the work of some linguists and sociologists who had not consulted him, and by giving me some reading 'homework' for our next 'class' he defined his role as an authoritative teacher of a naive pupil. As teacher, I believe that he perceived himself as both mentor and censor of the innocent's ethnographic knowledge.

At the end of our fourth interview, Nii Kofi introduced a new dimension to our relationship by inviting me to accompany him to a meeting of the Ga royal family council which was discussing the selection of a candidate for the stool. Since the meeting was conducted in Ga, all the aural communication I received was mediated by Nii Kofi. This invitation, however, initiated a new aspect of our relationship, in which he arranged for me to observe the sequence of ceremonial surrounding the enstoolment of the new chief, the life crisis rites of members of his extensive kinship network during my stay in Ghana, the cycle of traditional religious rites revolving around the cultivation of millet. Accompanying me to these events often involved considerable dislocation in his personal life; more than once we met at 4 a.m. to attend a ceremony; once it was after 2 a.m. when I left him at the gate to his compound; after one entire day spent in a sequence of ceremonial meetings in different Ga towns, he was so physically exhausted that he had to be carried out of the car to the house. That the invitations continued and increased, however, depended in part upon my meeting certain tests of competence. For example, wanting assurance of the reliability and nature of my observations, Nii Kofi requested to see the notes I had taken at the first political ceremony we attended; fortunately, he was satisfied with his pupil's performance on that occasion.

An additional dimension to his role in our relationship was activated when I began to tape-record religious rites involving the use of an occult language unknown to my young research assistant. Then Nii Kofi also assumed the role of transcriber.

Although Nii Kofi occasionally withheld information by professing ignorance on a subject which weeks or even years later he discussed freely, he never consciously distorted information and openly acknowledged the limits of his knowledge, especially during my second field trip. Although such integrity was an inherent aspect of his personality, it related also to his definition of my potential role as an accurately authoritative communicator of information that he had gathered over the years.

In retrospect, the critical issue in my relationship with Nii Kofi was the development of trust. From the outset he appeared genuinely co-operative with my inquiry; only as our relationship matured did I begin to perceive the extent of his reservations, which I believe were never fully dispelled. Clues to the sources of his initial mistrust occurred in our first interview when we debated the use of such terms as 'tribe' and 'clan', which for him had pejorative connotations. After we had worked together for several months, he first acknowledged openly his mistrust of Europeans, while laughingly affirming that I appeared to have some respect for Africans and their ways of life. At a later date, he again articulated this issue and again affirmed that he perceived me as different. Yet while he eventually gave me his own field diaries and his uncle's diary, introduced me to his wives and children, involving me in their joys and sorrows, paved the way for me with political and religious authorities, he still refused to reveal himself in the form of an autobiographical recording. Thus to the end his trust was guarded.

Apart from testing my reliability, which undoubtedly occurred more often than I knew, two occurrences stand out as critical and transforming in our relationship. The first occurred at the end of my first research trip; I became aware of the second on my return to Accra.

Toward the end of my first research trip to Accra, I invited various people who had helped me in my research to a party at my house. Preparations included hiring a bus to transport the guests from Central Accra to the university and assembling soft drinks, gin, and cookies for about forty people. While I had envisaged the party as an informal afternoon gathering in Western style, it turned out quite otherwise. More people arrived than I anticipated, including a major chief and a high-ranking priest, with their retinues. While I certainly had not intended to seat forty people, there was no question of seating sixty; sufficient chairs, however, were found to seat the major dignitaries. Nii Kofi assumed the role of master of ceremonies, insisting that I make formal Ga greetings to the guests, which were followed by appreciative speeches and libations by the chief and priest. Our supply of refreshments was barely sufficient, even with the unexpected gift of cupcakes from Nii Kofi's daughter-in-law. When the bus finally departed for Accra, I was emotionally exhausted. The following day Nii Kofi upbraided me for having assembled insufficient chairs and refreshments when I had invited 'more than forty people'. Testily I replied that while in Ga culture all guests were customarily seated, in my culture at such afternoon gatherings guests usually stood; this appeared to be a novel idea which Nii Kofi accepted gracefully, but I knew that he perceived this as a failure, and I felt the distance in our cultural assumptions keenly. Although such reality testing was an unfortunate note on which to end a productive guardian-innocent relationship, it was also salutary for the innocent to discover the depths of her innocence.

During the three years between my first and second visits to Accra, Nii Kofi and and I corresponded occasionally. In his letters he related the latest births, marriages, and deaths within his family and our circle of mutual acquaintances, sent me dates of ritual events, answered my ethnographic queries, requested money for his youngest daughter's school fees, commented on manuscripts I sent, and rejoiced in the birth of my third child and the completion of my thesis.

When I returned to Accra, the first person whom I went to see was Nii Kofi. I found him at his son's new house, so weak that he was unable to leave the house at all. From others I heard that he had hidden this information from me lest I decide not to come. But while he was physically feeble, his mind was as alert and inquiring as ever and he occupied much of his time with laboriously writing a Ga encyclopedia. Nii Kofi's inability to leave his house necessarily transformed the content of our relationship. On the one hand, I felt freer to visit him frequently; on the other, I needed someone to fulfill his former roles as intermediary and guide. To some extent, he continued to play these roles by sending members of his household to bring people with whom he thought I would want to talk to his house. In the second of my precious three months, our relationship was further transformed by my realization that Nii Kofi's role as conveyer of information had been essentially completed, for my inquiry had gone beyond the limits of his ritual knowledge. Yet I felt under an obligation to maintain the relationship, though his guardian role had become reduced essentially to translator for the transcription of events recorded elsewhere.

Thus far I have described my understanding of the developmental processes involved in my relationship with Nii Kofi, but not what seemed to me the rewards of that relationship for him. Although I gave him certain material goods in return for his assistance, including paying for the printing of an article in 1965 and a television set in 1968, I do not think that these were the meaningful rewards from his point of view. Rather I think that initially in the role of teacher he enjoyed giving authoritative instruction to an innocent pupil whom he came to hope would publish reliable and respectful information about Ga culture. His role as guardian also enabled him to reactivate and establish relationships within his community at a time in his life when his social world was contracting. Finally, I think he took pleasure in discussing at leisure matters of interest to him which did not interest the people with whom he usually interacted.

In summary, my relationship with Nii Kofi began as a simple

informant-ethnographer relationship, expanded rapidly into a multiplex guardian-innocent relationship as our mutual trust developed, and contracted to an increasingly limited relationship between translator and transcribing innocent due to unavoidable physiological processes of ageing affecting his ability to play a more multiplex role. The limited relationship of translator-innocent was maintained not only for its ethnographic utility but for its positive affective meaning to both guardian and innocent.

Ataafio: Conscientious Miracle Seeker

Looking back it seems appropriate that on the cloudless mid-January day that I first walked into Ataafio's compound in the heart of Central Accra, I should have found him reading an occult magazine published in Philadelphia. At the time I was attempting to interview Ga adults in sixty houses in Central Accra; his house happened to be among the sixty. As he responded to my questionnaire inquiring about his own, spouses', children's, parents', and siblings' educational, occupational, marital, reproductive, and residential histories, I learned that he was a healer who had once assisted a psychologist in his research.

When I met Ataafio, I had been considering inquiring into the kinds of people who went to healers and the kinds of problems they presented. Given his past research experience, Ataafio seemed to be a potential guardian to this endeavour. Consequently, the following week I returned to inquire about his willingness to assist me. As Ataafio mixed some herbal remedy for barrenness on his back doorstep, he agreed to spend two afternoons each week with me collecting medical case histories from other healers. Before I left, I had agreed to send to Los Angeles for a magic mirror advertised in an occult journal.

As I came to know Ataafio, I learned that he had had a varied occupational career. After completing Standard VI in Accra, he joined the Salvation Army as an evangelist in Nigeria. After experiencing some ill-defined racial insult from a European Salvation Army official there, he returned to Ghana, where he became a clerk in a store. After a time he determined to become a healer, apprenticing himself for four years to an old practitioner. After completing his medical training, Ataafio returned to live in the house of a maternal kinsman in Central Accra, where he had lived for many years. Ataafio's formal religious affiliations had been as diverse as his occupational experience: raised as a Methodist before joining the Salvation Army, he later belonged to several separatist 'spiritual' churches in Cape Coast and Accra. Highly eclectic in his beliefs, Ataafio constantly sought new means of achieving psychic and physical strength. He was, in short, a conscientious miracle seeker.

Although the exact dating of events was essentially irrelevant to Ataafio's temperament, which delighted in superlative emphases, I think that he was in his late forties in 1964. A short, wiry, vigorous, gregarious man, he possessed not only a restlessly inquiring mind, but a strong will.

Although I as the innocent set the terms of our relationship more explicitly than I did with Nii Kofi, he as guardian expected more obvious tangible rewards for his assistance. Apart from the financial arrangements we had made for his weekly services, he made frequent requests for me to send away for 'super-scientific' books and paraphernalia; often at the end of the afternoon, he would ask me to drive him somewhere, such as the market or to a friend's house at some distance. Although I sometimes found such requests a nuisance, his services were valuable to me. Moreover, in the course of time, he came to value the knowledge he acquired through his guardian role (especially in 1968) and I know that he voluntarily acted to protect my interests as well.

Throughout its duration the formal structure of our guardian-innocent relationship was relatively constant, though its content and intensity changed. His guardian role was less that of a conveyor of information than that of a linguistic intermediary between me and others and guide to sources of information. Initially we were engaged for several months in collecting medical case histories; then as that project began to yield diminishing returns from my perspective, we turned to interviewing ritual specialists. As an interpreter Ataafio's main failing was a tendency toward exaggeration, though this could be monitored through tape-recorded interviews. In 1965, in response to his expressed interest, he accompanied Nii Kofi and me to a number of ceremonial events. In such triangular situations, he deferred to Nii Kofi's seniority and expertise. In 1968 when it was evident that Nii Kofi could no longer act as guide in the outside world, Ataafio assumed that role with vigorous enthusiasm and generous allocation of his time. Since I was inquiring into ritual aspects of his culture previously unknown to him and he was always seeking new ways of solving fundamental issues of human existence, he articulated the personal value to him of the information acquired and relationships established through his roles of guide and linguistic intermediary for me.

Nevertheless, I think that at heart our relationship was an instrumental one for both parties: he was useful to me; I was useful to him. While the connotations of utility expanded for both of us over time, it retained that basic core, in part because I defined and he accepted his role as intermediary to others and in part because we were temperamentally very different.

Awo Kai: Serene Cosmologist

Either Nii Kofi or Ataafio might have introduced me to Awo Kai, but while they shared my experience of meeting her, neither was directly responsible for it. When Nii Kofi and I began to discuss religious institutions, he mentioned the importance of song in Ga traditional religion; I asked if there was anyone who might sing for me and he replied that he knew a medium who might be helpful. When Ataafio and I began to record medical cases, one of the first healers we visited was Ataa Blofo. At our second interview Ataa Blofo offered to introduce me to one of his wives, a medium living in a village about ten miles from Accra. Ataafio and I arranged with Ataa Blofo to see her; when Nii Kofi heard of the projected trip, he said, 'She is the expert singer I mentioned to you'. So it happened that one February afternoon Ataa Blofo, Nii Kofi, Ataafio, and I drove together to Okaikoi village to visit Ataa Blofo's wife, Awo Kai.

On entering Awo Kai's compound, I noticed the luxuriant pot of ferns beside the doorway to her god's room, which contributed to the sense of gentle orderly calm pervading the compound and reflecting the personality and life-style of its owner. Awo Kai was not physically beautiful, though the serenity and warmth of her personality infused her otherwise unexceptional facial features. Like many older Ga women her body was bulky with large pendulous breasts, but the supple grace of her movements belied her size and age. In 1965 she probably was approaching sixty, her tightly curled hair was grizzled and her eyesight was failing slightly, but her skin was soft and smooth and her muscles were firm, tuned by a lifetime of dancing with the gods.

As I came to appreciate, this large awkwardly shaped but gracefully moving body housed an exceptionally magnanimous and intelligent personality. Awo Kai, a devout believer in an ancient tradition that she knew was passing, valued her role as medium of her god and considered herself an exceptional person, though her manner was unassuming. She was soft-spoken in a society in which people often spoke harshly. She possessed an inquiring intellect in a culture which did not foster speculative thought, particularly among women. She had the inner security necessary to be magnanimous about the virtues and failings of others. Her humour was gentle and her laughter infectious. She created the impression of a person at peace with herself and her world.

As she recounted her life, it was clear that this serenity was hard won. Looking back, she believed that she was always divinely blessed.

She said that the god caught her before she was born, for not only was her mother pregnant with her for seven years, but whenever her mother carried water from the river on her head, Awo Kai would become possessed in her mother's womb causing her mother to fall to the ground. Moreover, her birth was attended by a tumultuous rainstorm, which is a sign of divine favour and approval to Ga people. Throughout her childhood, the god made her ill, drawing her into a cherished relationship with her father who recognized her infirmity as a sign of divine favour, and into bitter conflict with her mother, who resented the expensive care required by this sickly, sensitive, and shy child. In her late teens Awo Kai married a farmer in her village and after his death she married Ataa Blofo. Although Awo Kai married twice and conceived several times, all her pregnancies miscarried — a singular affliction in a society evaluating women through their childbearing. Awo Kai attributed her misfortune to the jealousy of her god.

After her first miscarriage, Awo Kai said that she wandered into the bush three times. Each time she disappeared for several weeks, but she remembered neither what she did nor where she went, for a person has no memory of periods of possession. After her third return to the village in a violent thunderstorm, Awo Kai's vocation as a prophet was recognized. In order to avert the negative consequences of unpredictable and often unwelcome prophetic utterances, the god was entreated to permit her to become a medium, who only invokes spiritual beings at the request of supplicants. The role of medium enabled Awo Kai to resolve the personal conflicts engendered by her identification with her father and her barrenness, for mediumship transcends all other social statuses for those who believe that divinity may descend to earth and speak through living persons. Moreover, Awo Kai became not merely a medium, as many Ga women do, but an exceptionally esteemed medium known throughout the Ga community for her unsurpassed ritual knowledge. With esteem came financial success and ultimately the appreciation of her mother. Through her vocation Awo Kai achieved not only the respect of others but inner serenity.

On the afternoon that I met Awo Kai, she spoke very little, leaving most of the conversation to Ataa Blofo, but she posed for a picture and agreed to sing some religious songs for me the following week when she would be staying with Ataa Blofo in Accra. Several times in the following months, Nii Kofi and I went to Ataa Blofo's house to record Awo Kai's songs and to discuss their meaning with her. Since Awo Kai did not speak any English, Nii Kofi's role as linguistic mediator was essential; he performed this role with scholarly precision and courteous grace. Although I valued my early relationship with Awo Kai, it was a very limited one restricted to the recording and interpretation of religious songs.

When I returned to Accra to investigate the cult to which Awo Kai belonged, I expected that she would be a valuable conveyor of information, but I did not fully anticipate how valuable. Awo Kai not only spent many hours at my request discussing Ga religious beliefs and symbolism either at her house in Okaikoi with Ataafio or at Nii Kofi's house in Accra, but invited me to accompany her to many rites and to historic shrines in the forest. Our relationship changed from one in which I as the innocent initiated limited expeditions into her world into one in which she as the guardian invited me to travel as far as the limitations of my understanding permitted. In retrospect, two circumstances underlay this transformation in our relationship. At our first meeting in Nii Kofi's house, Awo Kai expressed her wish that the outside world should know about Ga culture as it did about other Ghanaian cultures and her hope that through me she might achieve this goal. Although she wanted to make this commitment to my work, she had reservations about the trust that she was placing in me by revealing information which should not be disclosed outside the religious community of believers. At our second meeting in Okaikoi, Awo Kai suggested that the topics which we discussed were so esoteric that I should offer a sheep to placate the gods; the following week, Ataafio and I brought a sheep to Okaikoi which she sacrificed. I think that the sacrifice of the sheep conveyed to her my respect for her work, for she never again raised explicitly the issue of the dangers associated with revealing the undisclosable.

In her guardian role, Awo Kai was primarily a conveyer of information. But the information which she conveyed was richly diverse. I learned about cognitive concepts through interviews about the attributes of divine beings, cosmogonic beliefs, and ritual motifs, or when we discussed the meaning of rituals I had observed her perform. From her I also gained some insight into the emotional meaning of her religious experience, as we walked through the forest, which I found was to her alive with spiritual and historical significance. Besides being a direct conveyer of information, Awo Kai also mediated information gained elsewhere, as she reviewed and amended other singers' songs and interpretations with Nii Kofi and me.

Toward the end of my stay in Ghana, an impending crisis in our relationship was averted through Awo Kai's magnanimity, Ataafio's concern, and Nii Kofi's tact. The critical issue was an appropriate gift for Awo Kai's services to me. On several occasions Awo Kai expressed her wish to give me land in Okaikoi so that I would be sure to return; I assumed that this offer was simply a gracious gesture and not to be considered seriously. One day, however, Ataa Blofo mentioned to Ataafio that Awo Kai wanted to give me land and that I should buy enough cinder-blocks for a four-room building; such an undertaking far exceeded my limited financial resources. Unknown to me, Ataafio went to Nii Kofi to ask how this problem should be resolved. Both Ataafio and Nii Kofi grumbled that the house project emanated from Ataa Blofo and not from Awo Kai. Nii Kofi determined that the best plan of action was for him 'to speak gently' with Awo Kai and explain my limited financial resources. The next time Nii Kofi met Awo Kai and me, he raised the issue of the gift and she magnanimously replied that I should give her whatever I wished. Subsequently Ataafio told her that I wanted to give her some money with which she could buy blocks if she wished. Then, on the day before I left Ghana, Nii Kofi, Ataafio, Awo Kai and I met at Nii Kofi's house where I presented my gift to her through Nii Kofi, which she graciously accepted.

In my guardian-innocent relationship with Awo Kai, her role was consistently that of a conveyor of information. The transformation that this relationship underwent was essentially that of expanding the contexts and kinds of information conveyed. Beginning in 1965 the relationship centered solely around religious songs, in 1968 our interaction increased, involving many lengthy interviews, observation of diverse religious ritual at her invitation, day-long treks through the bush to ancient Ga sites. Although our relationship was always linguistically mediated by Nii Kofi or Ataafio, their presence did not interfere with her willingness to communicate; the presence of additional people did inhibit her unless they were members of her household in Okaikoi. Once when we went to the site of an ancient Ga town with some other Ga people, I was distressed by her unwillingness to answer questions that ordinarily would not have been problematical; the next day when only Ataafio and I were with her, she initiated discussion of the very topics that the day before she had rejected. So she taught me not to inquire but only to observe until we were alone with Ataafio or Nii Kofi. Although our relationship was always mediated due to my linguistic incompetence, it was one from which guardian and innocent both derived great personal pleasure.

Conclusion

I have attempted to describe the dynamic processes of three personally important guardian-innocent relationships in which I participated as an urban ethnographer. On such relationships the success and also the weaknesses of an ethnographic study rest, for the guardians' perspectives necessarily shape the innocent's understanding of their social and cultural systems. Different sets of research questions, different guardians, and different innocents may produce variant profiles of the same small-scale community as the Tepotzlan and Pueblo studies have so eloquently demonstrated. How much more likely are such selective distortions in rapidly changing urban contexts. Although awareness of this problem is the initial step towards its amelioration, its eradication is impossible, given the nature of innocence and guardianship.

BIBLIOGRAPHY

General

Banton, Michael, *West African City*, London: Oxford University Press, 1957.

Barnes, J. A., *Marriage in a Changing Society*, Rhodes-Livingstone Paper 20, 1951.

Bascom, W., 'Urbanism As a Traditional African Pattern', *Sociological Review* 7 (1959): 29–43.

Colson, E., 'Family Change in Contemporary Africa', *Anthropology and Africa Today*, Annals of the New York Academy of Science, 96: 641–52 (1962).

Curley, Richard T., *Elders, Shades, and Women*, Berkeley: University of California Press, 1973.

Epstein, A. L., *Politics in an Urban African Community*, Manchester: Manchester University Press, 1958.

—— 'The Network and Urban Social Organization', *Human Problems in British Central Africa* 29 (1961): 29–62.

—— 'Urban Communities in Africa', in Max Gluckman (ed.), *Closed Systems and Open Minds*, Edinburgh: Oliver and Boyd, 1964, pp. 83–102.

Evans-Pritchard, E. E., *Nuer Religion*, Oxford: Clarendon Press, 1956.

Geertz, Clifford, 'Ritual and Social Change: A Javanese Example', *American Anthropologist* 59 (1957): 32–54.

Gluckman, Max, 'Tribalism in Modern British Central Africa', *Cahiers d'Etudes Africaines* 1 (1960): 55–72.

—— 'Anthropological Problems Arising from the African Industrial Revolution', in Aidan Southall (ed.), *Social Change in Modern Africa*, London: Oxford University Press, 1961. pp. 67–82.

Greenberg, Joseph H., *The Languages of Africa*, Bloomington: Indiana University Press, 1966.

Gugler, Josef, 'Life in a Dual System: Eastern Nigerians in Town, 1961', *Cahiers d'Études Africaines* 11 (1971): 400-21.

Gutkind, Peter C. W., 'African Urban Family Life', *Cahiers d'Études Africaines* 3 (1962): 149–217.

—— 'The African Urban Milieu' in Peter J. M. McEwan and Robert

B. Sutcliffe (eds.), *Modern Africa*, New York: Thomas Y. Crowell, 1965, pp. 332–47.

——— 'Network Analysis and Urbanism in Africa; the use of micro and macro analysis', *The Canadian Review of Sociology and Anthropology* 2 (1956): 123–31.

Hammond-Tooke, W. D., 'Urbanization and the Interpretation of Misfortune', *Africa* 40 (1970): 25–39.

Hance, William A., *Population, Migration, and Urbanization in Africa*, New York: Columbia University Press, 1970.

Lamphere, Louise, 'Ceremonial Co-operation and Networks: a re-analysis of the Navajo outfit', *Man n.s.* 5 (1970): 39–59.

Lévi-Strauss, C., 'The Future of Kinship Studies', *Proceedings of the Royal Anthropological Institute for 1965*, pp. 13–22 (1965).

Little, Kenneth, *West African Urbanization*, Cambridge: Cambridge University Press, 1965.

McCall, Daniel F., 'Dynamics of Urbanization in Africa'. in Simon and Phoebe Ottenberg (eds.), *Cultures and Societies of Africa*, New York: Random House, 1960, pp. 522–35.

Marris, Peter, *Family and Social Change in An African City*, Evanston: Northwestern University Press, 1962.

Mayer, Phillip, *Townsmen or Tribesmen*, Cape Town: Oxford University Press, 1961.

——— 'Migrancy and the Study of Africans in Towns', *American Anthropologist* 64 (1962): 576–92.

Miner, H, 'The Folk-urban Continuum', *American Sociological Review* 17 (1952): 529–37.

——— *The Primitive City of Timbuctoo*, New York: Anchor Books, 1965 ed.

Mitchell, J. Clyde, *The Kalela Dance*, Rhodes-Livingstone Paper no. 27, 1956.

Murdock, George Peter, 'Cognatic Forms of Social Organization', in G. P. Murdock (ed.), *Social Structure in Southeast Asia*, Chicago: Quadrangle Books, 1960. pp. 1–14.

Newcomb, Charles, 'Graphic Presentation of Age and Sex Distribution of Population in the City', in Paul K. Hatt and Albert J. Reiss, jr. (eds.), *Cities and Society*, Glencoe: Free Press, 1959, pp. 382–92.

Oram, Nigel, *Towns in Africa*, London: Oxford University Press, 1965.

Parsons, Talcott, 'The Kinship System of the Contemporary United States', *American Anthropologist* 45 (1943): 22–38.

Pauw, B. A., *The Second Generation*, Cape Town: Oxford University Press, 1963.

Radin, Paul, *Primitive Man as Philosopher*, New York: D. Appleton and Co., 1927.

Schwab, William B., 'Oshogbo: an Urban Community?' in Hilda Kuper (ed.), *Urbanization and Migration in West Africa*, Berkeley: University of California Press, 1965. pp. 85–109.

Smith, M. G., *West Indian Family Structure*, Seattle: University of Washington Press, 1962.

Southall, A. W., 'Introductory Statement', in Aidan Southall (ed.), *Social Change in Modern Africa*, London: Oxford University Press, 1961, pp. 1–66.

Soyinka, Wole. *The Jero Plays*, London: Eyre Methuen, 1973.

Turner, V. W., *The Forest of Symbols*. Ithaca: Cornell University Press, 1967.

Watson, William, *Tribal Cohesion in a Money Economy*, Manchester: Manchester University Press, 1958.

Wilks, Ivor, 'Tribal History and Myth', *Universitas* 2 (1956): 84–6, 116–18.

Wilson, Monica and Archie Mafeje, *Langa*, Cape Town: Oxford University Press, 1963.

Ghana

Armstrong, C. W., 'A Journal of a Century Ago', *Teachers' Journal* 9 (1937): 4–10.

Bosman, William, *A New and Accurate Description of the Coast of Guinea*, London, 1705.

Dickson, Kwamina B., *A Historical Geography of Ghana*, Cambridge: Cambridge University Press, 1969.

Field, M. J., *Search for Security*, London: Faber, 1960.

Fortes, Meyer, 'Time and Social Structure: an Ashanti case study', in Meyer Fortes (ed.), *Social Structure*, Oxford: Clarendon Press, 1949, pp. 54–84.

Goody, Jack and Esther, 'Cross-cousin Marriage in Northern Ghana', *Man* n.s. 1 (1966): 343–55.

Government Documents

1891 *Report of the Census of the Gold Coast Colony for the year 1891*, 1891.

1902 *Report of the Census for the year 1901, Colony of the Gold Coast*. London: Waterlow, 1902.

1907 *Proceedings Government Enquiry into Ga Constitution.*

1911 *Returns of Native Population in Towns and Villages of the Colony, and the Districts of Ashanti, 1911 Census*. Accra: Government Printer, 1911.

1923 *Census Report 1921 for the Gold Coast Colony, Ashanti, the Northern Territories and the Mandated Area of Togoland*. Accra: Gold Coast Government Printer, 1923.

1932a *Appendices Containing Comparative Returns and General Statistics of the 1931 Census.* Accra: Government Printer, 1932.

1932b *Report and Proceedings: Ga Stool Dispute,* 1932.

1947 *Town and Country Planning in the Gold Coast.* Accra: Government Printer, 1947.

1950 *The Gold Coast Census Population 1948: Report and Tables.* London: Crown Agents, 1950.

1955 *Report on Enquiry with regard to Friendly and Mutual Benefit Groups in the Gold Coast, 1954.* Accra: Government Printer, 1955.

1958a *Accra: a plan for the town.* Accra: Government Printer, 1958.

1958b *Proceedings Government Enquiry on Relative Position of the Nikoi Olai Stool of Djorshie We and the Frempong and Agbon Stool, in the Asere Division of the Ga State, 1958.*

1961 *Accra Statutory Planning Area: Detail Statutory Planning Scheme no. 1.* Accra: Government Printer, 1961.

1964a *Special Report 'A': Statistics of Towns.* 1960 Population Census of Ghana. Accra: Census Office, 1964.

1964b *Special Report 'E': Tribes in Ghana.* 1960 Population Census of Ghana. Accra: Census Office, 1964.

1971 *Special Report 'D'; List of Localities by Local Authority, Greater Accra and Eastern Region.* 1970 Population Census of Ghana. Accra: Census Office, 1971.

1972 *1970 Population Census of Ghana.* vol. II. Accra: Census Office, 1972.

Grove, David and Laszlo Huszar, *The Towns of Ghana,* Accra: Ghana Universities Press, 1964.

Henty, G. A., *March to Coomassie,* London, 1874.

Kaye, Barrington, *Bringing Up Children in Ghana,* London: George Allen and Unwin, 1962.

Meredith, Henry, *Account of the Gold Coast of Africa.* London, 1812.

Nketia, J. H. Kwabena, *African Music in Ghana,* Accra: Longmans, 1962.

Reindorf, Rev. Carl Christian, *The History of the Gold Coast and Ashanti,* Accra: Basel Mission Book Depot, 1950 ed.

Rouch, J. 'Migration au Ghana', *Journal de la Société des africanistes* 26 (1956): 33–196.

Ward, W. E., *A Short History of the Gold Coast.* London, 1935.

Wilks, Ivor, 'The Rise of the Akwamu Empire, 1650–1710', *Transactions of the Historical Society of Ghana* 3 (1957): 99–136.

Ga and Accra

Accra Municipal Council. 'Panel Members Association Research Committee's Report: Ga-Adangme and Akan Systems of Marriage', (MS), 1957.

Ackah, C. A., 'The Historical Significance of Some Ghanaian Festivals', *Ghana Notes and Queries* 5 (1963): 16–27.

Acquah, A. I., 'The Development and Functioning of Municipal Government in Accra', *Annual Conference Proceeding of WAISER*, 1956, pp. 97–8.

—— *Accra Survey*. London: University of London Press, 1958.

Addy, P., 'Report on Wages and Standards of Living in Accra', (MS), 1945.

Adefioo. 'Lecture on Accra to Cosmo Literary Club'. (MS), *c*. 1920.

Adjei, Ako, 'Mortuary Usages of the Ga Peoples of the Gold Coast', *American Anthropologist* 45 (1943): 84–98.

Allott, A. N. 'A Note on the Ga Law of Succession', *Bulletin of the School of Oriental and African Studies* 15 (1953): 164–9.

Amarteifio, G. W., D. A. P. Butcher, David Whitman, *Tema Muhean: A Study of Resettlement*, Accra: Ghana Universities Press, 1966.

Amaertey, A. A., *Adzenuloo*, Accra: Bureau of Ghana Languages, 1961.

Ammah, Charles, *The Ga Homowo*, Accra: Advance Publishing Co. Ltd., 1968.

Ammah, E. A., 'Social Organisation of the Ga People: A Review', *Daily Echo*, June 6-June 21, 1941.

—— *Infant Outdooring in Ga Society: Bi Kpodziemọ*, Accra: E. A. Ammah and Sons, 1958.

—— 'Annual Festival of the Ga People', *The Ghanaian* August: 9–11, September: 25–6 (1961).

—— 'Festivals of Gas and Jews', *The Ghanaian*, October: 20 (1961).

—— 'Ghanaian Philosophy', *The Ghanaian*, October-June issues (1961–62).

—— *Materialism in Ga Society*, Accra: Institute of African Studies, University of Ghana, 1965.

Amoah, Frank E. K., 'Accra: A Study of the Development of a West African City', unpublished M. A. thesis, Institute of African Studies, University of Ghana, 1964.

Berry, J., *Pronunciation of Ga*, Cambridge: Heffer, 1951.

—— *The Place-names of Ghana*, (xerox), 1958.

Boateng, E. A., 'The Growth and Functions of Accra', *Bulletin of the Ghana Geographical Association* 4 (1959): 4–15.

Brown, A. Addo-Aryee, 'Signs and Omens', *The Gold Coast Review* 2 (1926): 285–9.

Bruce-Myers, J. M., 'The Origin of the Gas', *Journal of the African Society* 27 (1927–8): 69–76, 167–73.

—— 'The Connubial Institutions of the Gas'. *Journal of the African Society* 30 (1931): 399–409.

Danniell, William F., 'On the Ethnography of Akrah and Adampe, Gold Coast', *Journal of the Ethnological Society of London* 4 (1856): 1–32.

Engmann, E. A. W., *Ganyobi*, Accra: Bureau of Ghana Languages, 1961.

Field, M. J., *Religion and Medicine of the Ga People*, (1937). Accra: Oxford University Press, 1961 ed.

—————— *Social Organisation of the Ga People*, London: Crown Agents, 1940.

—————— The Investigation of the Ancient Settlements of the Accra Plain', *Ghana Notes and Queries* 4 (1962): 4–5.

Fitzgerald, Dale K., 'The Question of Duo-locality Among the Ga: A Preliminary Study', (MS), 1968.

—————— 'Prophetic Speech in Ga Spirit Mediumship', (MS), 1970.

Fleischer, Rev. C. and M. B. Wilkie., 'Specimens of Folk-lore of the Ga-people on the Gold Coast', *Africa* 3 (1930): 360–8.

James Town Maternity Clinic, 'An Exploratory Survey of Values in Central Accra', (MS).

—————— 'Health Education and Community Mobilization in an Urban Community in Ghana: Preliminary Report Central Accra Community Health Pilot Project NIHMR/MOH', (MS).

—————— 'Oyarifa: A Survey of a Village', (MS).

—————— 'Report NIHMR/MOH Pilot Project Area: Social Structure Considered in terms of Community Health Programme', (MS).

—————— 'Social Survey Preliminary Report: Central Accra Community Health Pilot Project NIHMR/MOH', (MS), 1964.

Kilson, Marion D. de B., 'Ga and Non-Ga Populations of Central Accra', *Ghana Journal of Sociology* 2 (1966): 18–25.

—————— 'Continuity and Change in the Ga Residential System', *Ghana Journal of Sociology* 3 (1967): 81–97.

—————— (ed.) *Excerpts from the Diary of Kwaku Niri*, Legon: Institute of African Studies, University of Ghana, 1967.

—————— 'Variations in Ga Culture in Central Accra', *Ghana Journal of Sociology* 3 (1967): 33–54.

—————— 'Possession in Ga Ritual', *Transcultural Psychiatric Research* 5 (1968): 67–9.

—————— 'The Ga Naming Rite', *Anthropos* 63/64 (1968/69): 904–20.

—————— 'Libation in Ga Ritual', *Journal of Religion in Africa* 2 (1969): 161–78.

—————— 'Taxonomy and Form in Ga Ritual', *Journal of Religion in Africa* 3 (1970): 45–66.

—————— *Kpele Lala: Ga Religious Songs and Symbols*, Cambridge: Harvard University Press, 1971.

—————— 'Ambivalence and Power: Mediums in Ga Traditional Religion', *Journal of Religion in Africa* 4 (1971): 171–7.

――― 'Twin Beliefs and Ceremony in Ga Culture', *Journal of Religion in Africa* (in press).

Kropp, Mary Esther, 'European Loan-words in Accra Ga', (MS), 1965.

――― *Ga, Adangme and Ewe (Lomé) with English Gloss: Comparative African Wordlists no. 2*, Legon: Institute of African Studies, University of Ghana, 1966.

Manoukian, Madeline, *Akan and Ga-Adangme Peoples of the Gold Coast*, London: International African Institute, Ethnographic Survey of Western Africa no. 1, 1950.

Munger, E. S., 'Land Use in Accra', *Zaire* 8 (1954): 911–19.

Nketia, J. H. K., 'Traditional Music of the Ga People', *Universitas* 3 (1958): 76–81.

――― 'Prayers at Kple Worship', *The Ghana Bulletin of Theology* 2 (1963): 1–7, 19–29.

――― 'Historical Evidence in Ga Religious Music', in J. Vansina, R. Maundy, and L. V. Thomas (eds.), *The Historian in Tropical Africa*, London: Oxford University Press, 1964, pp. 265–83.

Nypan, Astrid, 'Market Trade; A Sample Survey of Market Traders in Accra', *African Business Series no. 2*, University College of Ghana, 1960.

Okunor, Vincent, *Tone in the Ga Verb*, Legon: Institute of African Studies, University of Ghana, 1967.

Ozanne, Paul, 'Notes on the Early Historic Archaeology of Accra', *Transactions of the Historical Society of Ghana* 6 (1962): 51–70.

――― 'Notes on the Later Prehistory of Accra', *Journal of the Historical Society of Nigeria* 3 (1964): 3–23.

Page, R. E., 'The Osu and Kindred People', *Gold Coast Review* 1 (1925): 66–70.

Peil, Margaret, 'The Apprenticeship System in Accra', *Africa* 40 (1970): 137–50.

Pogucki, R. J. H., 'Land Tenure in Ga Customary Law', *Gold Coast Land Tenure*, vol. 3. Accra: Government Printer, 1925.

Quarcoo, A. K., 'The Lakpa – Principal Deity of Labadi', *Research Review* (Institute of African Studies, University of Ghana), 3 (1967): 2–43.

Quartey-Papafio, A. B. 'Law of Succession Among the Akras or the Ga Tribes Proper of the Gold Coast', *Journal of the African Society* 10 (1910–11): 64–72.

――― 'The Native Tribunal of the Akras of the Gold Coast', *Journal of the African Society* 10 (1911): 320–30, 434–46; 11: 75–94.

――― 'The Use of Names Among the Gas or Accra People of the Gold Coast', *Journal of the African Society* 13 (1913): 167–82.

――― 'Apprenticeship Amongst the Gas', *Journal of the African Society* 13 (1914): 415–22.

—— 'The Ga Homowo Festival', *Journal of the African Society* 19 (1920): 126–34, 227–32.

Welman, C. W. 'James Fort, Accra, and Oyeni Fetish', *Gold Coast Review* 3 (1927): 73–88.

Wilks, Ivor, 'Akwamu and Otublohum: an Eighteenth-Century Akan Marriage Arrangement', *Africa* 29 (1959): 391–404.

—— 'Some Glimpses into the Early History of Accra', (MS).

Wright, V. 'Some Ga Customs', *Gold Coast Review* 3 (1927): 224–28.

INDEX